Don't Let the Kids Bite the Dog

A MEMOIR

KATHLEEN HOLSTAD PEASE

Copyright © 2018 by Kathleen Holstad Pease
All rights reserved

This book or any part thereof may not be reproduced or transmitted in any form or by any means, electronic or mechanical, including photocopying, recording, or by any information storage and retrieval system, without permission in writing from the publisher.

Library of Congress Cataloging-in-Publication data:
paperback
ISBN-10: 1974539008
ISBN-13: 978-1974539000

Product Lifecycle Management data:
Document Control Number: AR80-KP001-1
Revision: A

Editor: Geoff Young

Cover Design: Tracy Holstad Conley
Sketch Design: Gary Holstad, Tracy Holstad Conley
Layout: Jeff Pease, Dave Pease

An excerpt from this memoir was selected for publication in the Memoir Showcase Anthology 2018.

Manufactured in the United States of America
10 9 8 7 6 5 4 3 2 1

*I dedicate this book to
my courageous parents Lyda and Maurice Holstad,
and to my husband Carter for his constant encouragement.*

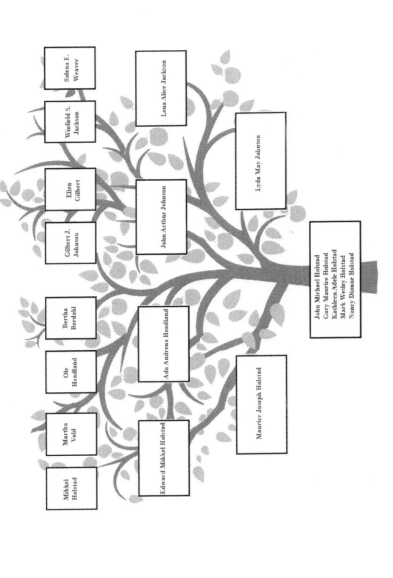

Contents

	Preface	ix
1.	Moles Trapped in a Den	1
2.	The Flying Nun	17
3.	The County Sheriff	23
4.	Martha's Trunk	40
5.	A Farm of His Own	53
6.	The Greatest Generation	65
7.	The Unexpected Gift	78
8.	Grandma and Grandpa Johnson's Farm	90
9.	Then There Were Four	102
10.	My Brothers, My Buddies	115
11.	May the Force be with You	122
12.	Let the School Bells Ring	142
13.	Small Town Living	159
14.	Starting Down the Slippery Slope	172
15.	The Eye of the Hurricane	184
16.	Off and Running	196
17.	A Whole New World	207
18.	Culture Shock	217
19.	On the Move	230
20.	Here We Go Again	241
21.	The Oldest Daughter	255

22. Buck Up, Buttercup 270
23. The Longest Year 279
24. Make Lemonade 301
25. Epilogue 306
    Acknowledgments 317

Preface

Oh! I will take you back, Kathleen
To where your heart will feel no pain
And when the fields are fresh and green
I'll take you to your home again!
—Thomas P. Westendorf

What is it about North Dakota that draws me? Was it my first experience with people? Was it the small, close-knit community in which we lived? Was it the modest life style and strong work ethic? Was it the challenging weather? Was it the fact that I left and the memories became better than the reality? For over 60 years, I've lived elsewhere—Portland, Mehama, Salem, Corvallis, Vallejo, San Diego, and Escondido—but my first thoughts on going home are always to Rolla, North Dakota.

Rolla has the force of a powerful magnet drawing me, yet I spent only eight years there. I've traveled back several times for family funerals and reunions. Each time, as I'd take a right at the Minot airport in my rental car and drive toward Rolla, the flat, straight roads laid out in a grid always took me back to geometry class and those 90-degree angles. Turn left at Rugby, the geographical center of North America, and I'm on my way.

The land was divided into quarters or sections as a result of the Homestead Act of 1862. The motivation to move to this arduous climate was the offer of "free" land to those brave souls stifled in other areas, often due to a lack of opportunity. My grandparents on my father's and mother's side were introduced to this area by the flyers that promised a better future in North Dakota. They came from Iowa and Indiana near the turn of the century looking for opportunity. They found a prairie with near-constant winds, fertile soil held together by thick grass, winters with blizzards and freezing temperatures warming only after spring approached. Summers were hot and often too dry or too wet for the crops, and thousands of grasshoppers insisted on being a part of it all.

As I make this trip today, the roads straddle the section lines. I pass farms en route to my grandparents' house, my heart pounding and my stomach churning at the anticipation of seeing the family farms and Rolla. The dry prairie winds and the hum of my tires are the only sounds breaking the country silence. It is calm and peaceful, so foreign from the cities I've just left.

Now I see Grandpa's shelterbelt—the tall trees swaying in the breeze and then the four grain storage bins. I turn into his yard and see the once-neat white house in desperate need of paint, the green composition roof faded and sagging. The two once-red barns now look tired and lonely, with the potato house just hanging on. Uncle Bill's house is still occupied and standing tall, proudly sharing the yard.

I continue driving and turn right to Aunt Pearl's house with sweet memories of eating her pancakes and popcorn, squeezing the squishy mud through our toes on those hot summer days, and the hours of playing Flinch with my cousins. A couple of miles and a few more turns and I'm at Aunt Ruth's place. The tree- lined entry is as impressive as always, and the stately red-and-white barn still dominates the property.

On I drive to Rolette, crossing the railroad tracks so important in my ancestors' decision to settle here. Proximity to a transportation hub brought homesteaders from other states and beyond. It doesn't take long to see Rolette now: the Farmer's Union, a cafe, a few stores, a couple of churches, and my cousin's bar. Continuing toward Rolla, I drive through Belcourt and the Indian reservation, where stories of Dad's years as sheriff come flooding back. Seven more miles to Rolla.

The grain elevators greet me as I cross more railroad tracks and begin the journey down Main Street. My excitement is hard to contain. There are so many emotions tied to this place. Oh, it's changed in sixty years, but the feelings come back to me. Fortune Martel's City Service gas station is gone, but our store is still here.

The wooden stairs that clung to the side of our brick building have been dismantled. The front door of the store has changed and the windows that Dad filled with the latest dresses and hats are gone. The store is now a bar that reeks of stale beer and seems to be a haven for disappointed lives. But I move on! The buildings on Main Street are older, but many are still familiar. My mind goes back to the fifties.

The school is on the same site, with additions to make it larger and more modern. I can still see where my first three classes were. Our basement house on the corner has become the foundation for someone's cozy home. Anne Dunlop's house is still a welcome sight and I imagine her standing on the porch.

I love this town, changes and all. It hasn't changed as much as I have. Where is that eight-year-old girl that was so free here? Ride your Hiawatha bike anywhere, be surrounded by people who know your parents and some who even know your grandparents. Ride fast and let the wind blow through your hair. Stop in and see a friend.

Is it possible to bond with a place? This was my cocoon. No freeways, no traffic lights, just streets with a few cars and people trying to get by. A simple town that I embraced.

Then in 1956, my world changed dramatically and often. My metamorphosis began as we moved to a new state, new schools, and a new life. The questions that haunted me and my siblings were "Are we there yet?" "Are we still searching?" "Can we stop now?" "Where is home?"

This is my memory of our story. Certainly, I cannot remember details of every incident or dialogue from the past. I have created conversations that illustrate stories I've heard or that I remember or that seem reasonable with the knowledge I have of the characters. Some of the events of my story are foggy, some memories no longer exist, and some are clear as a bell. How I would love to have just a few moments more with both parents to get the answers to some of my questions, but that's impossible so I'll do the best I can.

My goal is to preserve this history for the Pease boys: my sons Dave and Jeff, and my grandsons Alex, Nicky, Charlie, and Max. What makes us who we are? What can we learn by reading our ancestors' stories? Hold on to your hat! Let's find out!

1.

Moles Trapped in a Den

Rolla, North Dakota
1950

"North Dakota is so flat you can watch your dog run away from home for two weeks." —Jeff Foxworthy

"Why doesn't your house have a top?" my friend Shirley asked.

"It does," I said, pointing my finger toward our house. "Right there!"

"No, it doesn't! Look at the other houses. They have roofs that are up high."

I looked at my house as if seeing it for the first time. Shirley was right. My house was flat on top and the top was low to the ground. My house was different.

"The door to your house looks like a giraffe sticking his neck up," she continued.

Now I *really* looked at my house. Shirley was a year older than I was. She was already almost five.

We were standing on the corner of our lot right across the street from the school. Shirley lived kitty-corner from us in a house that looked just like houses in books. It was made of white boards and had two windows in the front. Its dark, sloped roof looked like a triangle from the side, and its front porch had four steps leading to the door. When you opened the door of Shirley's house, you didn't go down, you went straight into the living room.

I turned and looked at my house again. The top was flat and black, and Shirley was right: it did kind of look like a giraffe the way the door stood up above the flat tar paper roof of the house. When you opened the door, you walked down ten steps into our house. We had windows, but they were down on the ground if you were outside and at the top of the walls if you were inside.

"Actually, my daddy calls my house a basement house," I said. "Does your house have a basement?"

"Of course it does," said Shirley rather impatiently. "That's where you wash clothes. It's always kind of dark and cold down there."

"Well, our house is a basement house." I said, growing tired of this discussion.

"I think you should get a different house," Shirley said. "Your house looks scary after the snow melts and you can see that black top."

"I know, but if I got a different house, I wouldn't live by you."

We paused and pondered this unthinkable thought.

Then Shirley said, "I don't want you to ever move."

"Me either," I said. "Actually, I like my house."

"You do?"

"I do! When the snow starts to melt, water comes into our house and covers the floor. We get to wear boots and splash!"

"You do? I would like that. We never get water on our floors."

"When it happens next time, I'll see if you can come over."

"Wow! That would be great!"

"Yes! My house is really fun!"

Rolla, a town with a population of about 1,200, is a mere dot on a North Dakota map, located in the north-central part of the state. Just about ten miles south of the Canadian border, the house was sure to be covered with snow about nine months out of the year.

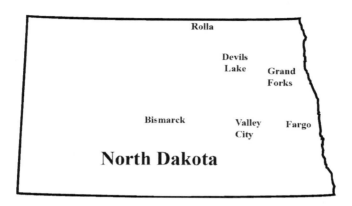

Shirley was right: why would anyone live in such a strange, scary, dark and damp house? My father began building the house when he returned to Rolla after his discharge from the Navy in 1944. He was eager to get on with his life. The long Alaskan winters, with the near-constant darkness and his yearning for Mom, meant he couldn't get home fast enough. He joined Mom in their small apartment in Rolla and slowly got to know my brother Jackie, now an active two-year old. Dad's former job at the Agricultural Adjustment Act (AAA) office in Rolla was waiting for him. The AAA was part of Franklin Roosevelt's New Deal. Farmers were paid to leave part of their land unplanted and kill excess livestock. The purpose was to raise crop prices by reducing quantity.

During Dad's deployment, my mother, Lyda Holstad, and Jackie would often drive the half hour to her parents' farm outside of Rolette to spend the weekend. Mom worked in Rolla as a case worker for the Rolette County Welfare Department.

With the war over, the folks were ready to have another child. Growing up, my mother was always close to her five siblings. Her parents, married for over fifty years, had a happy marriage. I don't mean they had an *Ozzie and Harriet* or *Leave It to Beaver* near-perfect life, but to have parents that liked each other through the many challenges of years of marriage is, I have come to believe, a huge gift. While the fifties song painted love and marriage as going together "like a horse and carriage," even as a child, I could see that some families were happier than others. My mom wanted to recreate the family she had grown up in and have several children of her own.

My father, Maurice J. Holstad, US Navy Photographer's Mate, Second Class.

My mother, Lyda May Johnson Holstad.

The Art Johnson Family. Top row: Cecil, Lyda (my mother), Ellen, Pearl. Front row: Bill, Art, Ruth, Lena. 1928.

Mom became pregnant soon after Dad's return. Their apartment in the Bateson House was clearly too small for a family of four, so the folks looked at other options in Rolla. Since there were few unoccupied houses in town, they decided to build a new home. Their savings account was small, building supplies following the war's end were often hard to come by, and dry summer months to build a home in Rolla were limited, so they would build a home in steps. Step one was purchasing the corner lot across from the school.

Step two was to complete the basement, which would serve as a temporary home until more funds became available. The key word here is temporary, at this point an undefined amount of time. A hole was dug for the basement, and mortar and concrete blocks were used to build the walls. Concrete was a fairly new product on the market following success in war applications. Small windows about 17 inches high were placed at ground level. Above the windows was the flat, level roof covered with black paper and tar which would eventually become the ground floor. As Shirley had pointed out, not a charming home yet, but one that provided room for our expanding family.

The basement was ready in November 1945, just in time for Gary's birth on December 9. Gary was a happy baby and the folks were thrilled to have another child. Jackie stepped up to the "big brother" role, and the family adjusted to their new underground home.

Sketch of a Basement House.

Eighteen months later the excitement continued, as my father brought my mother and me home from the hospital in their seven-year-old, forest green 1940 Ford. A new baby, and this time it's a girl! Dad pulled back the pink blanket to reveal my bald head and wrinkled face and introduced me to my brothers.

"This is your sister, Kathleen," he said.

Jackie looked on with interest, while eighteen-month-old Gary smiled and said, "Gong Gong!"

Dad tried again, "This is Kathleen."

Four-year-old Jackie got it. He responded, "Kathleen!"

Gary continued smiling and said, "Gong Gong!"

I was less than a week old and Gary had changed my name forever. A few days earlier the folks had finally gotten to use their carefully selected girl's name Kathleen. Not Kathy, but Kathleen. The popular song "I'll Take You Home Again, Kathleen" rang in their ears as they proudly said the name. Gary's toddler interpretation, however, would take precedence. From that point on, I was known as "Gong Gong" and as the years continued, I became Gong—that is, to everyone except my father. He always called me Kathleen.

Jackie, age 3, feeding Gary, age one month, 1946.

Fast-forward to 1966, my sophomore year at Oregon State University, and my future husband is approaching me to ask me out on a date. "I'd like to invite you to the movies, but do I have to call you Gong?" The answer was "Yes!" and fifty years later, he's still calling me Gong.

In no time, living underground had become the norm. The boys had their own bedroom, and I slept in the crib in my parents' room. We had a small living room, a bathroom, and a kitchen. A utility area with tubs fastened against the wall for laundry and children's baths stood next to the darkroom. My father was a photographer's mate in the Navy and photography would be his passion for the rest of his life so he created a tiny closet-sized darkroom.

Bath time for Jackie and Gary.

From our basement view, the windows were at ceiling level. There were days when Mother complained of feeling like a mole trapped inside this underground den with three young children.

During my first month my parents were concerned about my frequent and loud cries. This was not the precious little girl they were expecting, and many times that month they would gladly have switched me for a calmer, quieter model. My crying continued. Soon Gary began toddling over and clinging to Mother's apron, while Jackie stared off into the distance, fondly remembering those golden days when he was an only child. I was content if Mother held me, but as soon as she put me down, the screeching noise returned.

Kathleen at six months.

Mother was a modern woman and chose not to nurse, feeding all of us formula instead. After checking with the doctor, she changed from formula to a Karo Syrup recipe that soothed my stomach. That, coupled with the fact that I had discovered the bliss provided by sucking my thumb, quieted me down somewhat.

Dad would often set up his camera and studio lights in our cramped living room to document his growing family. He would put a solid color blanket on a table and have us pose for pictures. We have some real gems from those years.

Dad started an aerial photography business with a friend who owned an airplane. On weekends, he would photograph farms as his friend buzzed over them and then he'd return home and print 11" x 14" black-and-white photographs in his darkroom to sell to local farmers. This endeavor added to the family coffers and also allowed my father to pursue his favorite hobby.

A couple of years ago an eBay query on Maurice J. Holstad found two of his farm photos from 1947, on sale for $20 each. Of course, I bought one. The black-and-white photo shows a white, two-story North Dakota farm house surrounded by a barn and a few outbuildings, a shelterbelt, or windbreak, and then the level fields. The crops were planted in horizontal rectangles of varying tones of gray, like a neutral patchwork quilt, dividing one farm from the next. The credits state: "Sky Views, J.S. Amble, pilot. M.J. Holstad, photographer. Altitude: 250 ft. Rolla, North Dakota".

Meanwhile, back in the basement house, my brothers soon became my idols. I watched as they played with cars and trucks on the basement floor. As soon as I could crawl, I began grabbing their toys and relishing our time together. They had a different view of it, of course.

Mother's initial excitement at having a girl included visions of pink dresses and dolls, but her excitement dwindled quickly as she asked each of us what we wanted Santa Claus to bring. The boys had studied the Sears, Roebuck and Co. catalog and Jackie responded, "A truck or a train!" Gary answered, "A dump truck!" My answer was simple, "Truck." My mother couldn't stand it. Santa fulfilled the boys' wishes and brought me a truck and a small doll.

Kathleen's first birthday.

When the walls of the basement house started to close in on my mom and all three of us wanted to play with the same truck, we would hear, "You all need to go outside and get the stink off." In summer, she would send us up the stairs and out the door. In winter, she would spend twenty minutes bundling us up in several layers, adding a snowsuit and hat, and finally placing a scarf across our face.

Our neighborhood was male-dominated. The Dunlops lived across the street and down the road, while the Leonards lived diagonally across the street. At this time, the Dunlops had four boys and a girl, while the Leonards had two boys and a girl. The kids were about our ages, and we spent hours playing with them in the summer. I adored Janice Dunlop, who was Jackie's age. Shirley Leonard, just a year older than me, was my little pal. Anne Dunlop and Millie Mae Leonard became my mother's best friends. During the summer, they got together and talked. During the winters, the phone became their link.

On bright summer days, light filtered through the windows, bringing rays of sunshine down into our home. During the long North Dakota winters, mounds of snow covered the windows and our house was gloomy, feeling more like an igloo than a house. But this was our home, so we turned the lights on and played stories of our favorite heroes on the record player in the living room.

As our winter days turned into weeks and months, the ruthless North winds would howl and blow snow. Many winter days had temperatures below zero. North Dakota winter temperatures can get as cold as sixty-below-zero in the winter, while summer temperatures can rise to well over 100 degrees.

There were usually three or four major storms a year—often blizzards with powerful winds and low visibility. Winter usually began in October or November and ended in April or May, with an average snowfall of forty to fifty inches. Day after day, the isolation and bone-chilling weather made the first signs of spring a triumphant event.

Jackie, 6 years old: Kathleen 18 months: Gary, 3 years old.

When the temperature warmed and birds started returning to the area, we knew spring had arrived. We would cheer as the snow started to melt. Usually we had such a solid snowpack on the house that the melting process could take weeks, but the winter of 1949 was unusually long and cold. Before we could get too excited about spring, the melted snow seeped through our cinder block walls and our underground den became a lake.

Either the sealing for the walls was eliminated in the rush to get the house done, or it was just inadequate, but for whatever reason, we spent part of that spring paddling around the house in a few inches of water. We put our winter boots on and began splashing, which led to the inevitable wet clothes. Dampness permeated the air as the lower parts of our furniture were saturated and the house began to smell musty. We played on the beds to keep dry, watching with childhood glee as the random sofa pillow or our favorite toys floated by. Yes, my friend Shirley would love this, and what my mother needed was another child to share this adventure!

Needless to say, my mother was challenged by these living conditions. She usually had a good sense of humor and often laughed at our antics, but long days in this isolation tested her sanity. When we heard her tired voice say, "I'm going to trade you off for a dog and shoot the dog," we knew it was time to behave. She had reached her limit. Later, when I comprehended what she was saying, I thought she must be kidding, but I still heeded this warning because I was never quite sure!

Today, when a woman is pregnant you often hear about color schemes for the child's nursery and possibly purchasing a different home with a bedroom for each child. In the fifties, it was a different world. The deprivation created by the war was over, and the focus became the consumer and the family. Manufacturers previously producing products for the war now made appliances and household items never dreamed of a few years earlier. Through the benefits of the GI bill and government mortgage loans, veterans could purchase small basic homes for the first time.

My grandmother, Lena Johnson, on the left with a friend in front of the log cabin my grandfather Art Johnson homesteaded in.

My parents had grown up hearing stories of hardship and courage from their homesteading parents. This pioneering spirit was ingrained in them. The folks knew that temporary solutions often had to be endured until a goal could be achieved. Instant gratification was nonexistent. Hard work, persistence, and sacrifice were the name of the game. My family lived in our "temporary" basement house for five years.

2.

The Flying Nun

Rolla, North Dakota
1950

"When you are a nurse you know that every day you will touch a life, or a life will touch yours." —Anonymous

Our life in the basement was periodically interrupted by trips to the Rolla Community Hospital, just a block from our house and a modern facility for its time. The three-story brick structure completed in 1940 was a source of pride for the Rolla community. After all, it had the first and only self-service elevator in town, and it was a thrill for us each time we rode in it.

The hospital was staffed by Catholic nuns and the chief nurse was Sister Bertha. She'd sail down the spick-and-span halls with her white habit billowing behind her. Her garment was long and Casper-the-Friendly-Ghost white, complete with the band across her forehead and the sturdy, white cotton veil covering her head and shoulders. The starched fabric visor surrounding her face certainly must have limited her peripheral vision. She wore frameless round glasses, and the no-nonsense look on her face made even the boldest residents get out of her way.

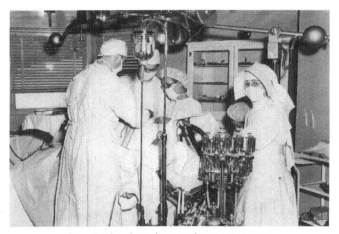

Sister Bertha taking charge in the operating room.

Four years earlier when my mother first experienced labor pains as Jackie was trying to enter the world, she was admitted to the hospital with her mother at her side. My father was completing his first year of Navy training and so Grandma was starring in the support role. Mom suffered through 36 hours of near-death pains under the watchful eyes of Sister Bertha. My mother was not a screamer, and as her contractions continued and then continued some more, my mother became dependent on this dedicated angel of mercy. Sister Bertha gained respect for Mom, and for the rest of our years in Rolla, the friendship these two established would bode well for the entire family.

In this era, childhood diseases were just a part of the preschool years. In the fall of my second year, I had a mild case of whooping cough. The next year, during a two-week period, Jackie, Gary, and I all had chicken pox. In March of the following year, 1950, Gary had stomach pains that were diagnosed as appendicitis, and later both Jackie and Gary had their tonsils removed. Of course, they were hospitalized and operated on, but often we spent time in the hospital for reasons that are very minor by today's standards.

The month after Gary returned from his surgery, my mother noticed that the nail around my index finger was red and tender. She had me soak it in an Epsom salt solution, and when it didn't get better, she took me to Dr. Miles. He examined it and recommended that I be hospitalized so the nurses could put hot packs on my finger. Are you kidding me?

I was admitted to the hospital, where I was put in an oversized white metal crib with very high side rails: Think old movies showing orphanages like *The Cider House Rules*, where they have rows of these enormous institutional cages without a top. I remember sitting in this Baby Huey-sized crib that was out in the hall on the second floor, yearning for my family.

In spite of the hot pack treatments, my infection persisted. The next day, I was wheeled to the operating room, put on a table with a huge, bright light shining down on me, and then "put under" with ether. Did they have no one else to operate on?

"It's slow in surgery today. Hey, the little Holstad girl's finger is still infected. Let's remove the nail!"

Now, I'm not saying that was the conversation, but it could have been.

I was terrified when a black rubbery mask was put over my mouth and the cold ether spray hit my face. There was no time to dwell on this, however, because I was suddenly "out" and when I came to, I was back in the giant crib with my right hand wrapped in yards of bandage material. Somewhere in the operating room there was an extra baby fingernail.

I had no idea where I was until I noticed the metal crib rails. My hand was the size of a baseball mitt with the layers of gauze bandages on it and I started screaming. I looked up as Sister Bertha came flying down the hall with her veil flapping in the breeze to see what the problem was. Here was the original flying nun racing toward me, and she was scarier than my sore hand and that horrid bright light in surgery.

Thankfully, my mother arrived about this time to rescue me. She picked up the red-faced screaming bundle, quickly created a hole in the layers of gauze, and found my thumb. As soon as my thumb was in my mouth, I was a happy girl. She put me back in the crib and, sucking for dear life, I drifted off to sleep! Sister Bertha breathed a sigh of relief as another medical crisis was averted on her watch.

Kathleen at age three.

A year later, I had tonsillitis. It was the typical sore throat, runny nose, and a fever, but the fever grew higher each day. Two days earlier, the doctor had given me a penicillin shot, but when my fever persisted, I was admitted to the hospital. My mother and I met Sister Bertha in the hall. Sister Bertha inspected my hand to make sure there was nothing that would keep me from my comforting thumb and then assigned me once again to the giant crib in the hall.

I really did not feel well this time, so I barely reacted when I saw the crib from Hell sitting there. I just put my favorite thumb in my mouth and went to sleep. I was three now, but my thumb was still my best friend. After a couple more days of high fevers and near constant sleep, mother got a call from the hospital, "Lyda, Kathleen has broken out in a rash and we would like to discharge her immediately. When can you come?"

My mother was suddenly alert, "What is the diagnosis?" she asked.

"She has the measles and she needs to go home!" came the quick reply. The hospital was now contaminated. Sister Bertha had a weary look on her face as Mom said her goodbyes and carried me home.

3.

The County Sheriff

Rolla, North Dakota
1951

*"There are only two lasting gifts we can give our children:
one is roots, the other is wings."* —Anonymous

Our new home was magnificent: a two-story stucco building complete with small fenced front yard and a walled walkway joining the house to the Rolette County Courthouse. The total structure seemed immense. Granted, mine was the viewpoint of a three-and-a-half-year-old, so ideas of size and scale should be tempered.

It was a crisp morning in January 1951. My family was moving from our basement house into the sheriff's house. The previous November, my father had been elected sheriff, and my two older brothers and I were thrilled. Unlike our basement house, the sheriff's house had windows. Large, rectangular windows. We could observe the changes in the weather, watch cars drive by, wave to neighbors, and enjoy the light filling the house. What were the chances? All of this and a jail in Dad's office, which was part of our house.

Certificate of Election.

That week, the *Turtle Mountain Star* reported the following:

> The new Rolette County Sheriff, Maurice J. Holstad must have felt like a bus driver without a bus when he moved into the Sheriff's quarters last Saturday to begin his official duties. Much like Mother Hubbard, when Sheriff Holstad took over custody of the county jail, there was not a single wrong-doer confined to the

cells and the prison was bare. However, it didn't take long for business to start as the new sheriff confined a prisoner at 2:30 AM Saturday.

The sheriff's house was built in 1903 and was Rolla's primary school house until 1910, when the new school was built.[1] At some point, it became the residence for the county sheriff. The living room, dining room, and kitchen shared the first floor with Dad's office and the jail. We all slept upstairs. My brothers shared a bedroom. The house had a renter named George from the previous sheriff's term, and my parents agreed to let him stay. George had a bedroom at the end of the hall next to the bathroom. My father's tiny darkroom was next to my parents' bedroom at the front of the house. I shared their bedroom, with my twin bed tucked in one corner.

My dad was the sheriff of Rolette County, which meant he was paid to maintain law and order in our county consisting of four or five farming communities and the Belcourt Indian Reservation, just seven miles from Rolla. Crimes in our county were usually drunken driving, disturbing the peace, or petty theft.

My forty-two-year-old father was a stoic Norwegian, a second-generation American. He was a man of few words, but often when I entered the room, his upper lip, outlined by a pencil-thin mustache, would turn up on the ends and

---

1. *A History of Rolla North Dakota*, 1888-1988

I'd get a wink that conveyed the love he couldn't put into words.

He was a fit man, six feet tall and weighing less than 200 pounds. I thought he was very handsome in the gray fedora hat he seldom left at home. He had a good feel for his jurisdiction. I often heard him say, "Anyone can make a mistake and get into trouble."

The Sheriff's Office. Back row: Jackie, Reed Mathews (Dad's friend from his Navy days), Maurice holding Kathleen. Front row: Lyda and Gary.

My father's office in the back was the official part of the house. It had its own side entrance with a glass window in the door that stated in large black letters: Sheriff's Office. Across the office was another door that went into the breezeway where my father could quickly walk to the courthouse for meetings and trials. Directly behind his desk was the jail. The door to the jail was made of thick metal and was almost always closed. When there were no prisoners in jail, my father would open the heavy door and let me help him clean the ten cells.

The jail was an intimidating and lonely place with a unique stale smell. There were a couple of small windows near the ceiling which probably explained why even with the lights on, it was always subdued, as if twilight was an all-day affair. As exciting as it was to be in this normally forbidden place, I was always happy to return to the pleasant office and close the door behind us when our tasks were complete.

I was envious that both of my brothers were in school. I couldn't wait to go. This was Gary's first year at school, and I had two years to bide my time until I got to go. I already missed Gary so much. School seemed like a magical place to me with the small tables and chairs, shelves of books, and wooden puzzles. Kindergarten and preschool were nonexistent in Rolla—maybe they hadn't been invented yet. During the day, I was welcome in my father's office if just he and his deputy Ernie were there, but if I heard unfamiliar voices, I knew not to open the door from our living quarters.

A two-way radio occupied a large portion of my father's desk. This was his link to law enforcement officials throughout the state and our link to my father and Ernie if they were out in their cars. The radio was leading-edge technology for the 1950s. My father spoke into a standing microphone on his desk. Our call sign was KAD908, and when I heard that from his desk speaker, I would run to get my father if he wasn't in his office.

When my father was out chasing criminals, my busy mother would sometimes let me call him on the microphone and relay her messages. When we heard a call from him, she would ask me to go into his empty office and respond. These times were high points in my days because they made me feel important and useful.

When my dad was busy at his desk, I could walk next door to the courthouse to visit Luba Johnson in her first-floor office. I would slowly open the heavy door with Superintendent of Schools etched in the glass. If Luba was working at her desk, she would pause and say, "Hello Kathleen. How are you today?" I loved her!

She was so nice. She knew I enjoyed books and she had a wall filled with all the textbooks the school district was using. I would find the first-grade books and pick a couple I liked, and she would check them out for me. With books in hand, I would go up and down the courthouse stairs and see what was happening in each office that had an open door.

Then I would return through the breezeway connecting the courthouse with the sheriff's office and spend a few hours enjoying my books. I couldn't read, but I could look at the pictures.

Deputy Sheriff Ernie Fortin and Kathleen.

Dad hired Ernie Fortin as his deputy. Ernie and his wife Alice were longtime Rolla residents with two grown sons. Ernie worked part time to give Dad a break from his duties, and we quickly became friends.

My mother was responsible for cooking the prisoners' meals. She had a limited county budget to buy their food and she also had little interest in cooking. She was busy taking care of the house and her three children. She viewed cooking as a means of providing nourishment to our bodies and was lost without her can opener. Grocery shopping meant bringing home lots of canned food.

She was a whiz at preparing cold Van Camp pork and beans, grilled Velveeta sandwiches, Campbell's cream of mushroom soup, tuna casserole, Spam sandwiches, scrambled eggs, and red, green, yellow, and orange Jell-O. During the war, there were food shortages and rationing, but in this postwar period new foods such as margarine and boxed cereals had been introduced. Convenience foods like cake mixes were beginning to appear.

Both of my parents were active in the social activities of our small town. Dad was a member and former commander of the American Legion and was somewhat active in the Masons. Mother belonged to the American Legion Auxiliary, the Eastern Star, a community study club, and the Homemakers' Club. During the long North Dakota winters these activities provided a means of socializing and getting out of the house.

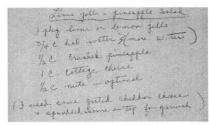

Recipes from Mom's recipe box, 1950's.

I loved to watch my mother get ready for various meetings. Sometimes she would wear her long white ceremonial gown for Eastern Star events. Those were my favorite nights. She would wash her naturally curly hair that was already almost all gray and use the bobby pins to make curls around her face. She would put on rouge, face powder, and lipstick. The best part was when she would spray her perfume, Evening in Paris, from the blue bottle.

Since her vanity was beside my bed, I could enjoy her beautiful smell long after she left and I was in my bed. On these special occasions, she would wear her high heels and I was spellbound. My mother was beautiful. When she went downstairs Dad's eyes would light up. He adored Mom and loved to see her looking her best. While taking care of us each day, she would normally be up early wearing one of her print house dresses. Her hair would be combed, but that was all the time she took for herself.

When we lived in the basement house, Edward Mikkel Holstad, my dad's father, stayed with us off and on as his needs for care came and went. He also spent some time in San Haven, the State Tuberculosis Sanatorium, located two miles north of Dunseith at the base of the Turtle Mountains. Grandpa didn't have TB, but was in and out of the Sanatorium as he aged since it was the closest medical facility to his farm.

In between times, he would stay with us. He enjoyed our antics, and we thrived on his attention as he sat in the big chair in the living room and watched us play. Grandpa had raised two boys, and since I was the first girl in the family and the baby, I enjoyed lots of time on his lap. He kept a comb in his shirt pocket, and I would take it out and comb his hair, sometimes bringing the comb onto his face. My mother would scold me. "No Gong. You can't do that. That hurts Grandpa's face. Look! It's red!"

I would look up, comb in hand, and study the red lines on Grandpa's face. He laughed and said, "It's fine. Kataleena is happy."

My mother disagreed: "Gong, you must not hurt Grandpa."

I put the comb back in his pocket. I needed to find a new game.

Mother also told the story that during those early years I had a dark green wool snow suit. She was shopping one day and found a white rabbit fur baby cap trimmed in the same green wool. She could just see it on me, but it was much too expensive. She came home and told the story at dinner, and Grandpa reached into his wallet and gave her the money for "Kataleena's" hat.

Grandma Ada Holstad passed away when my father was in the Navy in 1942, just two weeks before Jackie's birth. She was a strong woman who discussed politics with the men, including my mother's father, Grandpa Johnson. She drove the family car as Grandpa Holstad sat beside her in the front seat. She was a take-charge woman with a sturdy build, while Grandpa was a small man with a gentle soul. We never met Grandma Holstad, but she sounded intelligent and efficient, and she adored my father.

Kathleen in green snow suit.

Edward Holstad Family: Maurice, Harry, Edward, Ada.

A month after we moved into the sheriff's house, Grandpa Holstad died. He was eighty-one years old and had been in poor health for several years. This was my first experience with death, and I had a hard time understanding that this kind and gentle man was gone forever.

"Where did he go?" I asked. "Why can't he come back?"

My mother just shook her head and said, "Grandpa's body was getting old. It didn't work anymore. He was not feeling well."

"Oh no! Where did he go?"

"He went to Heaven. He's with God and we will all miss him."

I felt lonely, sad, and confused. Where was Heaven? One of my best friends had left me, but we didn't spend time talking about it.

Jackie, 5 years old, Grandpa Holstad, Kathleen, 1 year old, Grandpa Johnson, Gary, 2.5 years old. 1948.

Since my father's brother Harry did not have children, Jackie, Gary, and I were Grandpa Holstad's only grandchildren. His life on the farm was lonely after Grandma died. When he came to our house, he was often ill but always seemed to enjoy our company.

As we tried to comprehend our loss and the rituals associated with it, my parents prepared for the funeral and incoming guests. My dad's brother Harry and his wife Elsie were coming from Portland, Oregon, and Dad's Holstad cousins were coming from Iowa. They spent several evenings at our home, and we all enjoyed the new faces and the attention we received. When they left, they complimented the folks on their well-behaved children and even suggested that perhaps our family should include more children. My folks put that thought on hold.

The philosophy of disciplining children in the fifties was "spare the rod and spoil the child." In our family, Dad used to say, "I'll tell you once, but not a second time." If the second time was required, it was often reinforced with a spanking. Dad or Mom would turn us over their knee and give us a couple of firm swats. To avoid this, of course, we learned to respond fairly quickly when we were directed to do something. Both parents often said they were not raising "brats," which was our clue to step up to the plate and behave.

The County Sheriff

Edward Mikkelson Holstad's funeral, February 1951. John Holstad, Maurice Holstad, Harry Holstad (Dad's cousin), Roy Holstad, Mable Limesand, Elsie Holstad, Harry Holstad (Dad's brother). Children: Kathleen, Gary, and Jackie.

We drove to Grandpa Holstad's farm later that month to begin the process of getting rid of his possessions and selling his farm. This was Dad's third month as sheriff, and they had lots to do at home, but this was a weekend priority. As they were evaluating what to do with tools in the barn, my mother discovered an old trunk half hidden by straw in a dark corner. When she cleared the hay off its top she saw the hand-painted trunk. It was coral with blue rosemaling swirls accenting the black iron hardware that held the trunk together and had a slightly domed lid. Opening it, my mother found a black key about eight inches long that opened a lock on the front of the trunk. The trunk was rectangular, with two metal bands reinforcing its top and black iron handles on each end. In yellow, elaborately hand-painted letters, it was inscribed, *Martha Thor, Daller Wold, 1861.* The trunk was large and heavy, made of thick wood, with dovetailed corners.

Martha Wold Holstad's wedding trunk.

"Maurice, look at this trunk! It's amazing and almost 100 years old. This is incredible!" my mother exclaimed.

"Oh, that old thing came from Norway with my grandparents."

"Old thing? This is a work of art! Imagine the history. I wish it could talk so we could hear about the journey from Norway and then from Iowa to North Dakota."

Dad was only half-listening as he separated tools into piles for the upcoming sale: axe handles here, plows there, buckets piled next. My mother started moving horse harnesses and saddles into a pile. At the end of an exhausting and frigid March day, as we prepared to drive back to Rolla, Mother said, "We can't sell that trunk. It's a treasure."

My father frowned and said, "We never have extra room in our homes and it's so big. We need to sell it."

"Maurice, we must keep it. It is our only family heirloom."

"What would you do with it?" he asked.

"I could fill it with winter clothes in the summer and store summer clothes in it when it gets cold. We have never had as much room as we do now. It is really something."

My dad gave her that I'll-never-understand-women look and said, "When I come out Saturday, I need to take some tools back for your dad so I'll bring the trunk home then. If you change your mind, let me know. I really don't think we need it."

My mother never did change her mind, and the trunk resided in every house we lived in, always reminding us of our Norwegian heritage.

4.

Martha's Trunk

Rolla, North Dakota
1951

"And on the 8th day, God looked down at his planned paradise and said, 'I need a caretaker.' So God made a farmer." —Paul Harvey

"Mama where did we come from? Where was I before I was born?"

"I'm not sure where you were before you were born, Gong. You keep asking me that and I don't know the answer."

"Well, we had to come from someplace."

"Well, both Grandpa and Grandma Holstad's families came from the same area of Norway near a village named Vik. Grandpa Johnson's parents came from Norway, and Grandma Johnson's parents came from Switzerland. The trunk Daddy brought home last week from the farm originally came from Norway a long time ago. Norway is supposed to be a very beautiful country. Maybe someday you'll be able to visit it. Now I need to get dinner ready."

"Okay, but where was I before I was born?"

"That's enough Gong! Go play!"

Vik is located on the Sognefjord, about 100 miles from Bergen. This community is carefully tucked between the precipitous mountains and the water's edge in a defined space with no room to spare. During the 1800s Norway was dealing with the paradox of an increasing birth rate and the potato famine that was killing thousands. America suddenly looked like the land of opportunity.

The problem in Vik seemed to be a lack of resources to accommodate the growing population. Vik grew from 2,270 in 1801 to 3,230 in 1845. This was an increase of over 40 percent, and the resources of this confined, postage stamp sized area could not support the growth.[1] My great grandparents Mikkel and Marta Holstad left Vik for Iowa in 1867.

---

1. Odd S. Lovoll, *The Promise of America* (Univ. of Minnesota Press, 1999), page 24.

Vik, Norway
1867

It was 1867. Marta (Martha) Holstad paused and admired the view from her home. She never tired of the dramatic and stunning beauty of the Sognefjord. The steep, majestic mountains seemed to flawlessly flow down to the water, and the brilliant colors of blue, turquoise and green gleamed in the afternoon sun. Her children Tor (Tom) age 5 and Gyrid (Julia) age 2 were resting.

The view from Marta's window in Vik, Norway.

Marta Vold, 26 years old and Mikkel Holstad, 29, had married six years earlier and since then had lived with her parents, Thoe and Solveig Vold, on their farm in Vik. Mikkel was a tailor who also farmed to supplement the family income. Four Holstad farms were situated relatively close to each other on a ridge facing the fjord. They were just a short walk from one another.

Mikkel and Marta Holstad on their wedding day. 1861.

The Holstad farms had been established in the 1500s and now, over 300 years later, they were still producing as best they could. The steep mountains provided food, but the recent increase in population was taxing the village resources. Marta's father had always said to put your plow securely in the ground and hang on for dear life or you would be sliding down the slope into the house.

Marta was busy all day attending to her many duties, but during this brief quiet period, she tried to etch this breathtaking view into her brain. In a month, they would be emigrating to America and leaving all of this behind. Living in Vik was all she and Mikkel had ever known. The topography of the area left only limited space for the village between the fjord and the mountain slopes. Farmers were challenged to find creative ways to effectively use their steep land. To travel anywhere was at least a day's journey and a huge effort. The trail rose from the village up through the surrounding mountains. The easiest travel was by boat on the fjord, but those trips were few and far between. Soon she and Mikkel, with their precious children in hand, would travel to Bergen with their few possessions and board a ship for their month-long journey to Quebec, Canada.

They had received letters from friends who had already emigrated to America. Most settled in Iowa, where there were scattered Norwegian settlements throughout the state. It would be a relief to settle near other Norwegians since neither she nor Mikkel spoke English. The letters described a vast prairie with fertile soil covered with long grass. It was like a golden ocean, with the tall grasses swaying in the breeze imitating the waves of the Norwegian Sea. Mikkel was thrilled with the possibility of farming on flat land. Supporting two children on his income as a tailor was difficult and now in a few months they would be having another baby. Feeding the family was a constant challenge.

When Marta allowed herself to think about the crowded ship, the risk involved in crossing the vast ocean, and the trial thirty days on the ship would be for all of them, she grew anxious about the move. They would be traveling with at least 250 other passengers on the Bark (Barque) Brodrene, a three-masted sailing vessel. Hygiene was primitive, and disease could spread quickly in the confined surroundings. The ship's constant motion created nausea that for some of her friends had lasted the entire month. Weather was another uncertainty.

Once in Quebec, the family would have to travel to Iowa. The flat, fertile land allowed farms to be large, but could she live in such isolation from her neighbors? Mikkel had assured her he would try to find land close to town. Would their Norwegian ways seem strange to the Germans or Irish in the community? Would they be accepted?

The Holstads were a close-knit family, and Marta and Mikkel were leaving relatives they might never see again.

Mikkel's brother Anfinn would be going with them, which was a plus.

Marta's family, the Volds, were also dear to her. Her parents were talking about joining them in Iowa in a couple of years, which was most encouraging. With the overpopulation and limited opportunity in Vik, more friends and relatives might be coming too. "America Fever" was contagious.

They seemed to have no choice. When the risks seemed too high, Marta folded her hands and talked to God. "Please God, protect us as we make this drastic change."

Marta was organizing her wedding trunk in preparation for the move. It was large and sturdy and should be able to handle the journey. The coral-colored trunk had yellow, elaborately hand-painted letters that read: *Marta Thor Datter Wold 1861 (Martha Vold, Tom's Daughter 1861)*. Marta touched the gently curved lid and smiled. Her parents had given her this trunk on her wedding day. She never thought that in just six years she would be leaving Norway with it.

A knock on the door brought Marta back to reality. She opened the door to find Gudmund Brekke with his cart filled with the supplies she had ordered.

"Hello Gudmund! Thanks for delivering my goods up the hill."

"Don't mind making the delivery. Just don't make me leave Vik!" mumbled Gudmund. "Uff da, you won't get me going off to a new land. Vik is where I belong. I think you have lost your senses."

"Oh, Gudmund! Where is your faith? We can barely survive here. America means opportunity for us and our children."

"Well, that journey will be hard. Some ships sink, some people are sick the whole time. They get over there and just wish they were home. Family is important, you know."

"No one said it would be easy, but it wouldn't be easy to stay here either. Mikkel is a hard worker and I will help him all the way. We will do this! Now I'll see if Anfinn can help you move the supplies into the house. I have lots of work to do and the time to get started is now."

In a few short weeks, Mikkel and Marta glanced at the village of Vik for the last time. Their little family was starting the great adventure, and with tears in Marta's eyes, they journeyed to Bergen to board the Brodrene. There were 252 passengers on the ship including twenty from Vik.

The ship's passenger list shows Mikkel Johnsen Vold, Marthe Thorsdatter Vold, Thor Mikkelsen Vold and Gjori Mikkelsdatter Vold. According to Virgil Holstad, my father's cousin, Mikkel immigrated as a Vold since he had lived on the Vold farm. Once in the United States, the family reverted back to Mikkel's Holstad name. They left on

April 30, 1867, and arrived in Quebec just as planned on May 31.

During this period in history, Norwegian ships transported immigrants to Quebec and then took on loads of lumber to sell in Great Britain, providing profits both ways. Mikkel Holstad and his family arrived in Iowa, and the next year he purchased a 240-acre farm just two miles from Lake Mills in the north-central part of the state. Three more children were born in America: John, Edward, and Sylvia. Edward would become my beloved grandfather.

Mikkel Jonson Holstad Family. Back row: Edward, Tom, and John. Front Row: Julia, Martha, and Sylvia.

Martha's parents arrived in Iowa two years later. Martha resided on the farm she and Mikkel had purchased for nearly sixty years. Mikkel passed away on the farm in 1892. They were active in the Luthern Church and well respected in the community.

Lake Mills, Iowa
1900

Thirty-three years after Martha Holstad left Vik, she removed her prized possessions from the Norwegian trunk that had served her well and prepared to give it to her three youngest children. Land in Iowa was now expensive and hard to come by. Her children didn't want to leave their family and friends, and Martha could not imagine her life without them, but due to the Homestead Act, they could be landowners.

Flyers had advertised free land and rail transportation to North Dakota. Martha understood her children's misgivings at leaving an established community, but this was an opportunity that couldn't be missed. She could not let them see how she hated to have them leave. God would take care of them, just as he had taken care of her family coming from Norway.

So in the spring of 1900, the three youngest Holstad children, now adults, tried their hand at homesteading in North Dakota. John was thirty-three, Edward was thirty, and Sylvia was twenty-eight when they arrived in Dunseith, North Dakota, just a short drive from Rolla.

Edward, my grandfather, was successful in establishing a farm, and six years later he married my grandmother Ada Andrina Headland. Ada, nine years younger than him, was born in Fargo, North Dakota in 1879. Her parents Ole and Brita (Bertha) Headland had immigrated from the Vik area also.

Edward Holstad and Ada Headland on their wedding day, 1906.

I've traveled to Vik twice. Once in 2005 with twenty-six Holstads and spouses, all descendants of the Holstads that occupied the four farms on the ridge in Vik. The bulk of our group was from Iowa. My brother Jack, our younger sister Nancy and I represented the North Dakota Holstads.

Mikkel Holstad's restored home in Vik, Norway.

In 2017, my husband and I returned to Vik with good friends. Asbjorn and Linda Holstad live on one of the Holstad farms, and they graciously hosted us. A few years ago, Asbjorn restored Great Grandpa Mikkel's house, which stands next to Asbjorn's current home. Spending the night in this home that looked out on the fjord was a highlight of our trip. When we commented that we could not imagine ever leaving this view, he responded in his pragmatic way, "You can't eat the view."

5.

A Farm of His Own

Rolla, North Dakota
1894

"What you see depends on how you view the world. To most people this is just dirt. To a farmer, it's potential."
—Doe Zantamata

My future grandfather on my mother's side of the family tree, Art Johnson stood tall and proudly viewed the expansive prairie before him. Never in his wildest dreams had he thought he would be a land owner. He felt like his heart was going to explode. This was big sky country with flat and fertile ground, and this land would be his.

He had filed for this section of 160 acres adjacent to his father's section He would build a house and a barn, plant crops and raise cattle, have a life without a landlord. He would have a family. The possibilities seemed limitless.

How could change happen so fast? It was 1894, and he was twenty years old. This would be the best year of his life! He would work to earn money to build on this property and to plant crops. There was hope.

Gilbert Dvarkstein, Art's father and my great-grandfather, was a guild-trained tailor in Hallan, Norway, who emigrated to Wisconsin with his parents in 1845, when he was twenty-one. In Norway, the surname is often created by adding "son" to the father's name, so Gilbert changed his last name to Johnson since his father's first name was Johan (John).

Three years later he married Ellen Gilbert. Gilbert Johnson worked as a tailor until he and Ellen opened a hotel in New Albin, Iowa. Two years later John Arthur Johnson (Art), was born, their third child and first son.

By Art's tenth birthday, the family had increased to eight children. His mother was trying to cook for the restaurant, help run the hotel, and care for the children while his father suffered from a craving for alcohol that overshadowed his responsibilities as a provider. Fulfilling his role as the oldest son and with a fifth-grade education under his belt, Art quit school and worked for farmers in the area so he could give his fifty-cent weekly salary to his mother.

Art's formal education had ended, but his practical education was just beginning. Working with area farmers, he gained valuable experience and learned how to put in long hours of work each day. As he observed the farmers he worked for, he felt he would always be a farmhand. His family was having difficulty putting food on the table for all of the children. How could he ever own his own farm?

The Homestead Act of 1862, signed by Abraham Lincoln, provided 160 acres of government land to US citizens or intended citizens who filed an application, improved the land, and filed for a title.[1] The homesteader had to farm and live on the land for five years, and was required to build a dwelling measuring at least twelve feet by fourteen feet and grow crops.

Art's sister, Teo, and her husband, Lou Rice, were homesteading in the Rolette, North Dakota, area. Art's father, Gilbert, had received letters telling him about the land opportunities in the area, but also about the harsh winters. In 1892, Art and his father arrived in Rolette, and stayed with Teo.

Gilbert filed to homestead on land adjacent to hers. Art and Gilbert purchased a log cabin from a neighbor and moved it to the line between Gilbert's homestead and the parcel that would eventually be Art's. They planted cottonwood trees and added a sod house and a barn.

---

1. https://www.history.com/topics/homestead-act

Art's mother, Ellen, was fearful of Indians in the area so she and the rest of the children would not join them for seven years. Art borrowed tools from his relatives and worked for farmers in the area to earn money to improve his land and to buy his first team of horses in 1897.

The Gilbert Johnson Family, 1919. Back row: Teolina, Art, Oscar, Emma. Front row: Nettie, Gilbert, Lou Ida, Ellen, Annie.

Now here is the story of my Grandmother Lena. To promote their newly laid railroad lines, the railroads advertised excellent rates to North Dakota. For thirty-five dollars, a family could share a boxcar and bring one cow, two horses, and chickens. In 1898, Winfield Scott and Salena Elizabeth Jackson, my great-grandparents, traveled with their five children on an emigrant train to Rolla. Their oldest child was Lena.

Winfield was of Scotch-Irish descent. He had experience farming and working on the railroad. Lena's mother, Salena, was born in Switzerland and had immigrated to the United States with her family in 1857. The Jackson family of seven arrived in Rolla from Wabash, Indiana, in April 1898 and were surprised to find snow on the ground. Since the ground was frozen, they lived in their boxcar with another family until they could build a sod house on the land they would homestead.

Winfield Jackson and Salena Weaver on their wedding day, 1878.

The Winfield Jackson children. John, Harry, Lena (my grandmother), Bertha, and Ida.

Lena's father filed for a homestead just outside of Rolette, a small community about twenty-five miles from Rolla. He immediately began building a sod house for the family. They had to have a home before the severe winter winds began to blow. At nineteen, Lena, was a small-boned, pretty, and petite young lady weighing about 100 pounds. She and her oldest brother, Harry, went to the homestead plot to help their father build their house. A young man named Art Johnson was hired to help them. This was a real break for me.

"Opportunity is missed by most people because it is dressed in overalls and looks like work." —Unknown

Wood and stone were not readily available in this area so settlers used the soil of the seemingly endless prairie to build their sod homes. Art cut through the thick prairie turf with a plow. The sturdy grass roots were sliced into strips of sod usually three inches thick, twelve inches wide, and three feet long. They were laid in an overlapping manner to make walls for the one-story huts. Window and door openings were created and framed with poles. The roof consisted of poles placed across the walls, covered with a layer of tar paper, and then topped with more sod.[2] Packed dirt created the floor.

Not the lap of luxury, but this type of home was what my Grandmother Lena, her parents, and her siblings lived in, enduring the harsh winters and blistering hot summers. While they were living in the sod house, Grandma's brother

---

2. *A History of Rolla North Dakota, 1888-1988 (1988)*, page 23.

Bill was born. The Jackson family lived in this temporary home for eight years.

The sod house. Art Johnson is second from the left.

Lena loved learning and had completed the eighth grade in Indiana. With the encouragement of one of her teachers, she had taken a few college classes. After the sod house was complete, Lena attended a Teacher's Institute for a week in Rolla and completed her certificate requirements for teaching.

She began teaching all eight grades in a one-room schoolhouse in the area. She would arrive early each morning and light the fire in the stove, do the janitorial work, begin her teaching duties, and maintain discipline, which was sometimes a challenge since some of the eighth-grade boys towered over her.

Art began courting Lena during these teaching days. He continued to work and save money for his homestead. Three years after Lena's arrival, he went to Montana to work as a fireman on the Great Northern Railroad. Finally, on January 28, 1903, Art and Lena drove Art's horse and buggy to Rolla to get married. She was twenty-four and he was twenty-nine. They returned to Art's homestead and lived in the two room grainery while they built their home on the farm.

In 1905, their first son, Cecil, was born, followed two years later by their daughter, Ellen. Art was always interested in politics and in improving their community. He served as the Rolette County Commissioner for seven years and was then elected Sheriff of Rolette County, which meant the family had to move to Rolla.

Art Johnson and Lena Jackson on their wedding day.

By this time, they had two more daughters, Pearl, and my mother, Lyda. The family lived in Rolla for four years and then returned to the farm. While in Rolla, Bill and Ruth were born. The family returned to their farm near

Rolette, where Art and Lena lived the rest of their lives. Their children attended a one-room schoolhouse for their elementary years and then went into Rolette for high school.

My mother used to quote her father as saying, "Any damn fool can get married, but you need to be able to support yourself." He put his money where his mouth was and provided the opportunity for his six children, including four daughters, to attend college during the depression, when economic conditions could not have been more challenging. This was the man with the fifth-grade education.

Art had an abundance of common sense, a quick wit, a lot of character, and a strong work ethic. As the prairie winds were blowing the top soil off of his land during the depression, he was driving his high school graduates the 200 miles on trail-like roads to get their education at the Teacher's College in Valley City. He insisted that his daughters stay at Episcopal Hall since it was well supervised and provided religious training. Also, he wanted to support the Episcopal church since that was the church that had fed his family many times in Iowa.

My mother wrote:

> I graduated from high school in May of 1930 when I was sixteen, but the next month I turned seventeen. That fall, I went to Valley City to the Teacher's College

for two years. College seemed like a very big place to me compared to Rolette and I missed the farm and my family very much. The first year Dad picked me up for Christmas vacation and when we got to the big hill close to the home, I started crying and I cried all the way home. I had been so homesick at school. I had lost weight and I couldn't wait to see the family. I graduated with a two-year Standard Certificate in commercial subjects so I could teach typing, shorthand and accounting in high school. My dad felt that was the only way to get ahead in the world was to have a Standard Certificate or a college degree. All of us went to college for at least a year.

Ellen, Ruth, Lyda, Lena, Bill, and Art Johnson.

After college, my mother worked at various jobs in the Rolette County Courthouse in Rolla. She had a clerical position and eventually became a case worker for the Rolette County Welfare Office, making home visitations to welfare recipients in the county. She rented a room in Rolla and often returned on weekends to her parents' home, where she handled the accounting for the farm.

It was now the mid-thirties and everyone was suffering during those depression years. Mom's sisters were teaching in the area and for a couple of years, her dad had no money to pay the taxes on the farm. Farms were being bought by investors by just paying back taxes. Seeing that her dad had no money to pay taxes, my mother paid them for him. She remembered giving him the tax money for a couple of years and each time, he gratefully accepted the money with tears in his eyes. As economic conditions improved, Grandpa repaid the tax money to my mom. Years later, this situation would be reversed, as Grandpa would give money to my mom to help us create a new life.

6.

The Greatest Generation

Rolla, North Dakota
1926-1942

"Never in the field of human conflict was so much owed by so many to so few." —*Winston Churchill*

On a cold, windy winter day in Rolette in 1926, Art Johnson was in town buying supplies and picking up his children from school. He had six kids, two of whom attended Rolette High School. He slowly made his way to the front of the school, and Pearl and Lyda came running to the car. As they settled in for their ride home, Lyda said, "Do you know Maurice Holstad?"

Pearl nodded and said, "Yes, he's a senior."

Lyda continued, "I saw him today. He's cute!"

Pearl responded, "He's okay. He has kind of a big nose."

"He's tall and he looks nice."

"Yes, but he's way too old for you! He and his brother live in a shack."

"Why don't they live in a house?"

Art chimed in, "Their folks have a farm in the hills by Dunseith. They just stay in the shack during the week and go home on weekends. I visit his folks when I'm in the area. His mom knows a lot about politics."

Lyda was thirteen and Maurice was seventeen. In time, they would become my parents.

My mother was smitten with Dad the first time she saw him. He was tall and handsome, with a nice smile and kind eyes. He was quiet, but never seemed to miss a beat. He was a senior and had no memory of her during those years, focusing his attention on girls his own age.

Fast-forward a few years and Mom finally had his complete attention. She had become a tall brunette with naturally curly hair, a nice figure, and a sharp sense of humor. She was fun to be around and she appreciated his company.

My parents were married in 1940 at my mother's home. She was twenty-seven and he was thirty-one.

Maurice Holstad and Lyda Johnson on their wedding day, 1940.

In 1940, able-bodied men were being drafted into military service for World War II. Since most draftees were between the ages of eighteen and twenty-five, my father was hoping he would not have to serve. It wasn't that he lacked the patriotic spirit spreading throughout the country, but after going through the depression and the decade of the thirties struggling to find work so he and my mother could marry, he was ready to settle down and start a family.

My father was born in Kelvin Store, a post office and store operated by his father outside of Dunseith, North Dakota. It was located in the Little Prairie community about a half an hours drive from Rolla.

Kelvin Store.

His father, Edward Holstad, homesteaded in the area and married Ada Headland in 1906 at Kelvin. They had two sons: Harry, born in 1907, and my father, born in 1909. Harry was a gentle, sweet child and a slow learner. When my father was born two years later, his parents were thrilled that he learned quickly and was a calm personality, but more aggressive than his brother.

The boys grew up on a farm near Kelvin Store, so close to the Canadian border that part of their farm became the International Peace Garden when it was created in 1932. For many years it has commemorated the peaceful existence between the United States and Canada.

Maurice and Harry Holstad.

When the two brothers were ready for high school, the closest school was Rolette High School, about a twenty-five mile drive from their farm. The family didn't have a car to give them, and commuting would have been difficult anyway with the winter storms and poor roads so the boys lived in a small shack close to the school. My father skipped a couple of grades through promotions and graduated from high school in 1927, a year before Harry.

Timing is everything. The stock market crash of 1929 was the start of the Great Depression, limiting job opportunities for young men. You can imagine the excitement my father felt as he graduated from high school, and then suddenly the world was in an economic collapse, with no opportunities in sight.

The farmland in North Dakota had been overworked by the homesteaders that arrived thirty years earlier. There were few trees in the area and the soil was extremely dry. For years they experienced a seemingly never-ending drought. Crop yields were low and the prices for crops they did harvest were continually falling. Wells dried up and some people left, abandoning their farms and moving to cities to look for work. Grasshoppers or locusts arrived by the thousands and feasted on the parched crops. Fierce winds blew topsoil miles away, often damaging buildings in their way.

My mother's youngest sister, Ruth Olson, was ten when the stock market crashed. She remembers that no one had any money. She and some of her high school friends made dresses out of flour sacks. The government paid for and then destroyed herds of cattle that were starving since there wasn't enough grass to feed them. Deep pits were dug to bury or burn the carcasses.

Ruth continues:

> Looking off into the distance you could see grasshoppers coming up the roads and across the fields

like a big wave covering the land. There was nothing you could do. Everyone was scared and sad. Dirt blew day after day creating a dark cloud over the area physically and emotionally. Driving a car was possible only with windshield wipers on to clear the windows from the constant dust. Meeting a car on the road was very scary as the visibility was so poor. Dirt sifted in around windows and doors and no one felt clean.

The wind blew dirt and sand over the fence lines so cattle could just walk from one farm to another. During the summer, Ruth herded cattle on horseback every day. To control future soil erosion, farmers started planting shelterbelts to slow down the intense prairie winds.

My father's parents scrimped and saved so that in 1931, he attended Concordia College in Moorhead, Minnesota. He found room and board with a farm family living near the college in exchange for his work as a hired man. He was considering becoming a minister, but he could not finance another year in school, so he returned to his family home in Dunseith.

Maurice and his mother at their farm.

In 1933, frustrated with a lack of work in the area, my father hopped a freight train and ended up in California working on a Civilian Conservation

Corps (CCC) road construction project in Yosemite National Park. The CCC was a public work relief program for unemployed men ages seventeen to twenty-eight introduced as part of President Franklin D. Roosevelt's New Deal.[1] The maximum annual enrollment in the CCC was 300,000 men, and over time more than three million men participated in the program. They were given shelter, food, clothing, and $30 a month, $25 of which had to be sent home each month to families. At this point, my father was twenty-four so he didn't have long to be part of this program.

Dad returned to Dunseith in 1935 and eventually got a job in Rolla working as a clerk in the federal Agricultural Adjustment Act (AAA) office. Finally, in 1940, after both of my parents had been employed for a while, the economic climate was improving and on October 21, they were married. They rented an apartment in the Bateson house in Rolla and began their forty-nine years of marriage.

My father had now been out of high school for thirteen years, Mom for ten. They had endured the depression and witnessed economic collapse, unrelenting unemployment, devastating weather, and the undaunted strength of the individual. They were thrilled with their new life together and optimistic about the future.

---

1. http://www.history.com/topics/civilian-conservation-corps

Their idyllic married life came to a screeching halt one year later on December 7, 1941, when Japan bombed Pearl Harbor. That day changed the life of everyone! Suddenly, America became united as it had never been before or since. We had been attacked! Boys and men were enlisting in the armed services, women were volunteering for the Red Cross, and war bonds were a very patriotic means of saving money.

Since my father was thirty-two and my mother was pregnant, they were hoping he wouldn't have to serve, but the military needed him. He was about to be drafted, so in 1942 he joined the Navy. Following six weeks of boot camp at Great Lakes, Illinois, my father was selected to be a Photographer's Mate and was sent to Pensacola, Florida, for training. The photography training was a technical and creative experience for him. He learned about photo lighting, focus, and f-stops, as well as how to develop sharp black-and-white prints. For this farm boy from North Dakota, photography opened his eyes to a new world and became his passion for the rest of his life.

Maurice Holstad, aerial photographer.

Mom and Dad at Grandma Holstad's funeral, 1942.

A few months later, Dad's mother, Ada Holstad, died of a sudden heart attack. Dad was granted emergency leave to return home for a few days for her funeral, but then he had to return to duty. My brother Jack was born a week later, on November 21, 1942.

After completing his training, Dad was assigned to a Photography Unit in San Diego and wired Mom to come. This assignment was for the duration of the war. Mom was thrilled. She had hired Mary Hoffman, the daughter of her family's hired man, Bugs Hoffman, to take care of Jackie while she returned to work at the Welfare Office after Jackie's birth.

This was mid-1943 and to think that Dad would be assigned to San Diego for the rest of the war and they could be together was simply amazing. Mom spent most of her weekends with Jackie at her parents' farm and she couldn't wait to tell them.

"Mom, I'm going to pack everything I can fit into the car and drive to San Diego. Mary can go with me to take care of Jackie. Maurice will get to hold Jackie for the first time. I can get a job in San Diego. We are so lucky that he has been assigned to the United States and not off to Europe."

Her mother frowned and said, "You've never driven any real distance. Do you know how far it is to San Diego? Two women in a car with a baby? I know you want to be together, but this sounds crazy."

"Well, we are so fortunate to have our new car. It has great tires. Mary can navigate for me. It will be a long drive, but Maurice and Jackie and I will be a family. It will be fabulous."

The folks had purchased a 1940 Ford just before they got married, and that turned out to be a very wise decision. Laws were passed that forbade American auto manufacturers from producing cars from 1942 to 1945.[2] Retooling began immediately and auto manufacturing plants were suddenly producing bombs, tanks, airplanes, torpedoes, and other war munitions.

Grandpa Johnson came into the house just in time to hear the end of Mom and Grandma's discussion. "Of course, you need to go," he said. "You've got a good head on your shoulders and you need to be with Maurice. Do you have enough gas ration coupons? You'll get to see the ocean. I've always wanted to see the ocean. You go!"

---

2. http://teachinghistory.org/history-content/ask-a-historian/24088

Mom, Mary, and Jackie set out on their big adventure and did just fine. The reunion in San Diego was wonderful, but it lasted only a couple of weeks.

This was war time, and while Dad's aerial photography group gathered in San Diego, the powers that be grew concerned with Japanese activity on the Aleutian Islands, part of the US territory of Alaska. Japan had bombed and occupied the Aleutian Islands of Attu and Kiska. Was this the first step to another attack on our West Coast?

PBY, World War II. Official US Navy Photograph.

The United States quickly put together bases on the Aleutian Islands. Alaska needed to be defended and the Japanese needed to be monitored. Aerial photographers were needed to fly on reconnaissance missions in Alaska. You guessed it! In a matter of days, Dad's unit was flying to their new home in Adak, Alaska. He was assigned to a photography unit tasked with taking aerial photographs while flying in a PBY Catalina Navy reconnaissance plane. He would spend the next eighteen months in this desolate and frigid part of the world.

As quickly as Dad left, Mom, Mary, and Jackie packed their few possessions in their car and began the long drive home. Mom was deflated. Life in San Diego had been so short-lived. They would return to their apartment in Rolla, Mother would get her job back, and they would wait for the war to end.

7.

The Unexpected Gift

Rolla, North Dakota
1951

"In the military, you deploy for six months and then come home to safety. Police officers are deployed for 24 hours a day, seven days a week, 365 days a year." —Former Navy SEAL Chris Kyle

Let's press the pause button for just a second to recap where we've been. We started with my dad returning from war and the folks building a basement house. They increased the family size to three children and lived in the basement house for five years. Then my father was elected sheriff and we moved into the sheriff's house. Grandpa Holstad died and Martha's trunk was discovered, which took us on a long trip to Norway to meet my great grandparents. We journeyed back to America and eventually met up with my grandparents in North Dakota. We talked about how Mom and Dad met, and what *happened in the war years. Now the loop is closed and we are back at the sheriff's house ready to proceed with life. Only now, you know most of the family secrets, so sit back in your chair, put your feet up, and we'll figure out what the unexpected gift was.*

Saturday was the most exciting day of the week for our little town, as farmers and Indians came to socialize and get supplies for the next week. Conversations about the weather, the price of wheat and livestock, hunting, and fishing could be heard as men gathered on Main Street. Women stood in line at the grocery store enjoying time away from the farm gossiping, trading recipes, and discussing the child that was driving them crazy.

Saturday night was my father's busiest night. Teenagers from nearby towns would come into Rolla and drive up and down Main Street, checking out girls and squealing their tires around corners. If my dad saw them, he would pull them over and tell them to cut it out or he would call their parents. Everyone knew everyone in this small county, and the threat of calling a parent made even the most adventuresome drivers toe the line.

A few individuals would have too much to drink at the local bar and have problems driving home to their farm, or my father would get a call from the reservation, and by Sunday morning the population of the small jail had increased. It was always interesting to wake up and see who would be sitting around the breakfast table.

That summer, Gary and I decided to go out behind the house and play with our cars. We created towns in the dirt courthouse parking lot. Dad had two prisoners in jail that were waiting for Officer Benson from the North Dakota State Highway Patrol to take them to another county for trial. They had been with us for a few days, and to relieve the monotony of jail life, Dad let them carry the large jail trash can to the burn barrel behind the house. As we were playing, the two prisoners came outside dressed in their denim shirts and dungarees holding the handles on either side of the trash can. We looked up and watched as they walked to the barrel. All of a sudden, they dropped the trash can and ran toward the road in front of the courthouse. In a flash, Gary ran into Dad's office and said, "The prisoners escaped. They're running away!"

Dad flew out of his desk chair and came running out, with Gary close behind him. "Where did they go?" he asked.

I pointed toward the road and said, "They went down the road and turned right."

Dad said, "Gary, you stay out here and watch for them. Kathleen, go sit by the radio. I'll call when I find them."

The Unexpected Gift

Dad got in his car and sped toward the road.

Gary and I were both amazed that the prisoners would escape, and thrilled to be part of the excitement. Gary took his assignment seriously as he watched for any trace of the prisoners. I rushed into the office and sat at the desk with my heart pounding. This was unbelievable! Mom was busy upstairs, Jackie was at Donny Leonard's house, and Gary and I were helping our dad capture real live criminals. Who says a four- and six-year-old couldn't save the day? I had the microphone in my hand and waited anxiously for a message from my dad.

It was probably only minutes, but it seemed like hours in my small mind, before I heard my dad, gasping for breath and saying the magic words, "KAD908."

Sitting straight in my chair, I responded with my clearest voice, "KAD908, come in."

Dad informed me that he had captured the prisoners and he was on his way home. I rushed outside to tell Gary he could leave his post, then we both stood in the parking lot waiting for Dad to return.

In a few minutes he was back with both prisoners in the car. All three men were panting as they got out of the car, the prisoners now wearing handcuffs. Dad walked behind them into his office. Gary and I followed as Dad opened the jail door and gave the prisoners a shove. Dad locked the door and walked outside to get the trash can with a disgusted look on his face. Gary and I just smiled. This was the best afternoon ever!

Ernie Fortin, Reed Mathews and Maurice in the Sheriff's Office demonstrating techniques for capturing prisoners.

If we had several prisoners, my father would take their meals into the jail where the men would eat at a table in the middle of the room. When there were only a couple, it was easier to have them eat at our table and it was always a welcome diversion for us kids to have "guests" at meals.

One young man named Carol had run away from his home in Iowa and stolen a car elsewhere in the state. My father picked him up and brought him to our jail while he waited for Officer Benson (a friend, whose visits I always looked forward to) to take him back to the crime scene.

During his stay, Carol had endeared himself to Dad, so periodically my dad gave him a reprieve from jail and invited him into our house. We enjoyed having him at the table eating meals with us. He was like a big brother and seemed to thrive on our attention. He spent his time carving, so having a prisoner with a knife didn't seem to be a problem. He made a gunstock for Gary and taught Jackie how to play the harmonica.

Our favorite prisoner was an Indian named Buffalo. He was a tall young man, a Chippewa Indian, with coarse black hair and a sculpted face. He often shared the breakfast table with us, and to me, he seemed to be almost a part of our family. It was hard not to like him.

One night a few months earlier, as the wind blew and the snow swirled in all directions, the lights in the house and jail went out. Dad was out on a call, and Mom was in charge of the family and the jail. She said in a panicked voice that a fuse must have blown. The two-way radio that connected us to Dad in his car and the furnace fan that kept us warm in this thirty-below-zero weather were both dead.

"I don't know where the fuse box is in this house or how to fix this," she said as she ran her hands through her hair. There were several prisoners, including Buffalo, in jail that night, so she fumbled around in the kitchen until she found a flashlight. Then, making her way to Dad's desk, she found the jail key. She unlocked the massive door and called for Buffalo. He came out and she locked the door behind him.

"I don't know where the fuse box is, Buffalo," she confessed. "It must be here in the office." She shined the light up and down over the walls until we located the fuse panel.

"I can fix this," said Buffalo in a reassuring tone that made my pounding heart slow down.

He checked the fuses as Mom searched the bottom drawer of Dad's desk and found a box containing spares. As Mom held the flashlight, Buffalo replaced the fuse. Like magic, the two-way radio came to life, the room was bright, and the furnace fan whirled. Life as we knew it could continue.

Mom took a deep breath and began to relax as she patted Buffalo on the back and said, "You saved the day, Buffalo. Thanks!"

Buffalo nodded as Mom locked him back in jail.

The Unexpected Gift

That Saturday, I heard my father talking to Buffalo. "I wish you could stay away from the booze." he said. "It would sure make my life a whole lot easier and it would sure be healthier for you. After your night's sleep, you're a good guy to have around. Forget the Saturday night parties and just visit us when you're in town."

Buffalo looked down at his plate and sighed as he said, "I can never stop at one beer."

A few weeks later, I heard the metal jail door slam shut as I walked downstairs to breakfast. Normally I heard voices coming up from the prisoners around our dining room table, but today there was only silence. I had overslept. The sun was shining through the window, which meant my two older brothers were already at school. I was confused by the stillness of the house.

I entered the dining room just as my father came through the open door that connected our house with his office. He was carrying an empty metal tray. That meant he had taken the prisoners their breakfast and no one would be eating with us this morning. That was unusual, too. I was disappointed since I liked to eat breakfast with Buffalo. Each morning he would say, "Are you up to no good today, Kathleen?" That always made me smile.

My dad was frowning and as I got closer to him, I was shocked to see red-streaked scrapes and bruises on his face and arm. He had a large scratch across his cheek and the skin around one eye was almost blue.

"What happened to you?" I asked.

Dad frowned and sighed and then said, "Last night I got a call that Buffalo was drinking and causing problems on the reservation so I drove out to pick him up and he wasn't in the mood to cooperate. He was swinging his arms and caught my face, and the next thing I knew we were on the floor wrestling. He's in jail now so you might say I won, but when I looked at my face in the mirror this morning, I wasn't sure. On top of that, in the scuffle, I lost one of my gloves."

Now, as I looked at my Dad's bruised face, I couldn't believe Buffalo would do that. For the first time, I realized my father had a dangerous job. In the excitement of his election and the move to this big house, I had never thought of anyone hurting him. Roy Rogers and Gene Autry dealt with criminals all the time in the movies, and they never got hurt. In the constant pull of good versus evil, didn't the good guys always win? Buffalo was our friend. How could he hit my dad?

A few hours later, I was in Dad's office when an agitated, tired looking Indian woman flung the door open and stormed in. She was furious. She had long, thick gray hair and fire in her eyes.

She exploded, "You don't know me, but I am Buffalo's mother. You called him a 'son of a bitch' last night, and I am *not* a bitch!"

I didn't know what "son of a bitch" meant, but I could tell it wasn't good.

She continued with, "No one calls me that!"

My father's bad night was turning into his bad day. My stomach started to churn and my hands were sweaty as I watched from the office door while Buffalo's mother pointed her finger at my dad.

He sat down in his desk chair, looked up at her, and paused. He let out his breath slowly and said, "You're right. I was angry and trying to control your son, but I didn't mean to insult you."

He let out another tired breath and looked directly at her through his bruised eye and said, "I'm sorry!"

The little office was suddenly silent. It seemed like the whole world was standing still as I watched Buffalo's mother and wondered what would happen next. She paused and slowly nodded her head, accepting his apology. Then she turned and calmly walked out of the office with her head held high.

Time passed and eventually things returned to normal between my father and Buffalo. Dad had other cases to solve, and soon Buffalo had regained his seat at our table.

Winter was now upon us. Snowdrifts were almost door high in some places, and we all spent as much time as possible in the house. We were putting up our Christmas tree and my mother was baking cookies. The house was filled with the sounds of Bing Crosby dreaming of a White Christmas.

Playing in the snow. Jackie, Kathleen, and Gary. Sheriff's house, 1952.

The day before Christmas, my father returned to his office from a meeting in the courthouse to find a package on his desk. It was wrapped in blue and silver paper that had seen many Christmases before. My father picked it up and put it under the tree. On Christmas morning, we had the usual early morning rush to see what Santa had brought. When the excitement died down, my brother Gary found the blue and silver package and handed it to my father. He opened it, read the note, and smiled as he said, "Well, I'll be damned."

It was a pair of black, fur-lined leather gloves, something dear to anyone spending a winter in North Dakota. Attached to the gloves was a small note that read:

To the best Sheriff.
From Buffalo

Jackie's tenth birthday party at the Sheriff's house.

8.

Grandma and Grandpa Johnson's Farm

Rolla, North Dakota
1951

"Grandparents' house, where cousins become best friends."
—*Anonymous*

Once a month or so, if the roads were clear, Dad would drive us to Grandma and Grandpa Johnson's farm. As we turned onto the farm, the main road took us to the side door of their house. The front porch faced the main road and contained two elegant oval-glassed front doors, one opening into their living room and the other going into their dining room. I never knew why there were two doors and I don't remember ever using them.

Grandma and Grandpa Johnson's Farm

Grandma and Grandpa Johnson's farm.

This was the farm that my grandfather, Art Johnson, and his dad homesteaded in the late 1800s, but now it was 1951, so a few things had changed. The larger home once occupied by my great-grandfather and his family was now my Grandma and Grandpa's home. On the other side of the driveway, which was on the section line that originally divided the two properties, the former home of my grandparents was now occupied by my mother's brother Bill and his family. Bill and his brother Cecil farmed Grandpa's land. Just beyond Grandpa's house was the log cabin he and his father had lived in so many years ago.

My mother and her siblings: Bill, Lyda, Ellen, Pearl, Cecil, and Ruth, taken when Bill was home on leave. He served in the Army Air Corps during World War II.

Four of my mother's five siblings lived near the farm. In 1951, there were twelve of us grandchildren in the area and when we would arrive from Rolla, it was a chance for everyone to gather at Grandma's. The farm house quickly went from no children to twelve, and adding in the adults there were twenty-two of us when we got together. This was a minor invasion!

My mother's oldest sister, Ellen, and her husband, Warren, lived with their four children in Grand Forks. That was a couple of hours away so they couldn't come as often, but when they did, it was hard to find a seat in the house.

Grandma Johnson was a classy woman and her home had several elegant touches. It was always a mystery where they came from. The oval windows in the front door were lovely. Embossed beading accented the diamond shape of door knobs. A curtain on the downstairs bedroom door was made of a brocade-like wine-colored fabric, certainly not calico. The large kitchen table was always cleared and clean when we arrived, and the centerpiece was a cut-glass vessel holding silverware ready for the next meal. Grandma's china cabinet had glass windows that, I'm sure, were left with small fingerprints as we enjoyed gazing at the treasures inside.

Grandma homesteaded with her family from a farm in Indiana, lived in a boxcar for a time, helped build a sod house in which she lived with the seven other members of her family for years, and then moved to a grainery when she married

Grandma and Grandpa Johnson on their 45th wedding anniversary, 1948.

Grandpa, but the touches she added to her home were very refined. She used to tell of clearing fleas and other insects from her bed in the sod house before she could go to sleep. Some critters fell each day from the dirt roof of the small house with the help of the near-constant wind.

She was a small woman, not even 100 pounds, but she demonstrated her strength and stamina by running a home with six children and managing kids in eight grades as a young school teacher. In her quiet way, make no mistake about it, she was a force to be reckoned with. It was clear that she adored Grandpa. She enjoyed all of his stories and laughed at all the right places.

We always entered Grandma's house through the side door. After climbing up a few porch stairs, we'd open the tightly sprung screen door that closed with a bang as you entered a small mud room. On a winter's day, you would take off your boots here, being careful not to trip over the cream separator. From my four-year-old perspective, this was a tall, pewter-gray piece of equipment with a huge metal bowl at the top that Grandma put the freshly milked liquid into and then turned a crank that twirled it around creating a centrifugal force that separated the milk and the cream. The result was rich, thick heavy cream and almost blue-looking skim milk. Grandma would put the cream in a quart jar and she would often send it home with us. Eating our corn flakes the next morning topped with this magical substance made my mother say she had died and gone to heaven. If this was heaven, I would never be bad again!

We'd walk through Grandma's neat kitchen with the green painted boards framing the pantry and enter the living room. This was Grandpa's domain, where we'd hear "Don't let the kids bite the dog!" in Grandpa Johnson's booming voice as his tranquil Sunday afternoon was quickly becoming a hub of activity. He'd be sitting in his chair smiling at his cleverness, with his right ear close to the speaker of his console radio, larger than most of the first television sets. He was losing his hearing, so he always sat in his favorite chair with his back facing the entrance to the room. Often there was a Farmers' Almanac by his side as he studied the weather predictions and pondered what crops to advise his boys to plant. My uncles, Cecil and Bill, farmed wheat, barley, oats, and potatoes.

Grandma and Grandpa Johnson in their living room. Grandma is holding Jackie. 1944.

Grandpa was a staunch Republican and thrived on hearing the latest political bantering of both parties. He and Grandma had raised their six children and now, at age 77, he was slowing down. He had some heart issues and often used a cane.

Grandpa was a big man, over six feet tall with a wide frame. He didn't carry extra weight, but he had inherited his mother's broad hips. He had a sharp sense of humor, but was not a smiley man and certainly not a "let me hold you in my lap" type of Grandpa. With a stern look from him, we knew we needed to be quiet while he listened to the news on his radio.

Entering the living room now at age four, I'd grab mother's skirt and get my thumb in the ready position. The sound of Grandpa's voice sent a chill through my spine as he'd turn from the radio and say, "Oh God! Silence is back!" Then we'd hear the big laugh and my thumb would take up residence in my mouth.

I was his thirteenth grandchild and I was very intimidated by him. Actually, we all were. I said nothing in his presence, thus my nickname, Silence! I just stood there and stared. He enjoyed walking by me, bending over and pinching my dress, and then saying, "Very thin material!" I was mortified and he loved it!

Cousin Alyce Ann Johnson Lunde recalls that when Grandpa was washing his car and kids were watching him, somehow, without a pause, the rinse water would be splashed on his young audience and he would get a surprised look on his face. The cousins that lived closer to him remembered stopping by the house and eating toast with Grandpa in the morning. According to my cousin Dave Johnson, "It was always burned and it was the best toast I ever ate!"

When we were visiting one Sunday, my brother Gary remembers:

> I used to like to drive our car. Dad would let me steer as he worked the pedals out on the country roads. Grandpa found out that I liked to drive so he said, "Gary, let's go get the cows." Grandpa had a white 1950 Ford with one chrome bullet in the grill and we had a tan 1951 Ford with two bullets in the grill. I sat in Grandpa's lap and steered and we'd head out to the pasture to bring the cows in to be milked. Grandpa was working the pedals and I was steering and he would tell me to steer at a slow-moving cow and when we'd get close, he would speed up and bump into it and laugh as the cow started running. Then he would have me steer at another slow cow and bump into it and laugh, and that was the way we got the cows to the barn.

Cousin Linda Olson Tilton remembers:

> Grandpa scared me to death. The older cousins had told me that he was a "hanging Sheriff" and that fact really stuck with me. When he would 'guff' at me like he did, sitting in his chair with his back to the rest of the room, well, everything about him was pretty darn intimidating. He used to listen to this radio and we always had to be QUIET! I seldom went into the

living room. I just stayed in the dining room.

Visiting our cousins at Grandpa's farm was a real treat. As I grew older, I loved playing outside with them. We'd all gather together and play Pump, Pump, Pull Away or Prisoner's Base in Grandma's yard. The younger cousins would join in as they got older.

Tommy Thompson, Terry Thompson, Jackie, Dean Thompson.

Eventually, Grandma and Grandpa had twenty grandchildren. We were thrilled when our Grand Forks cousins could join us. There were four of us girl cousins close in age, and we would climb the steep stairs that started with three steps and then a sharp corner and it was a straight shot to the second floor. We'd play in the three upstairs bedrooms.

Our parents would gather in Grandma's living room, and they were soon exchanging news and laughing and enjoying each other's company. There was little attention paid to kids as we made our own entertainment. If we were all playing a running game outside, there would, of course, be disagreements over rules or who tagged who first, but by and large we settled our own problems.

Every once in a while if someone went into the house with a tear in their eye, a parent would appear to try to bring some adult supervision to the game, but usually the rule was figure it out, take your hits, and keep playing. We didn't want to bother our parents or have any supervision. To be labeled a "tattletale" was not a good thing. The group could turn on you. We ended up with scuffed knees or bruised arms at times, but we also gained some knowledge of how to get through life. There was a lot of humor in the group and we looked forward to this time together.

Richard Olson holding Bobby Olson, Tommy Thompson, David Thompson, Bill Leonard, Terry Thompson, Jackie, Dean Thompson, Gary. Wagon: Betty Thompson and Linda Olson, 1947.

If we got to stay in the evening, all the kids would gather in the kitchen for a game of Fruit Basket Upset. First, we had to determine who would be "it." One of the older cousins would line us up with both fists in front of us. They would tap each fist and count, "One potato, two potato, three potato, four, five potato, six potato, seven potato, more." If one of your fists was tapped as the leader said "more," that hand went behind you and we went through the process again. The last person holding out a fist was "it." That person would assign each player a name of a fruit and we'd sit in a circle on chairs. Then "it" would call out "Pears and Apples change places" and whomever he had given these names to needed to exchange seats without the person that was "it" getting one of their seats.

We would spend the evening laughing hard and making noise as Grandma's wooden chairs slid across the floor. We all hated to see the adults enter the kitchen and hear the dreaded words that it was time to go home. My uncles had cows to milk, and with regret, we drove back to Rolla.

Thompsons, Dunlops, and Holstads at Clear Lake, Canada.

9.

Then There Were Four

Rolla, North Dakota
1951-1952

"Parenting is a lot like folding a fitted sheet: No one really knows how the hell to do it." —*Anonymous*

"Mama, we need a baby! Janice Dunlop is going to have a baby to take care of and we should have one, too! My baby sister could play with Anne Dunlop's baby. Janice and I could give them buggy rides in the summer. I could help take care of my sister."

During the summer of 1951, Anne Dunlop announced that she was pregnant with her sixth child. As Anne's stomach grew, so did my insistence that we needed a baby. Obviously, our family had two boys, and when my sister arrived, we would have two girls. Such symmetry. Poetry in motion, you might say.

My mother had been preparing me for the fact that Gary would be starting school in September. Gary was my best friend and playmate. Without Gary, what would I do? I could continue to visit Luba in the courthouse once in a while, and sometimes I could accompany Dad during the day on his outings. I could visit Ernie and occasionally Officer Benson from the State Highway Patrol would stop by. But there were no children close by, and my mother explained that I had two years before I would be going to school. Two years was forever.

Of course, my mother had more time for me when the boys were in school. She took me with her grocery shopping, or when she planned baby showers or wedding showers with her friends. That meant I got to help make party favors by sticking big diaper pins in a large gum drop for plate decorations at baby showers.

Kathleen in the Sheriff's house, 1952.

Sometimes I got to go with my mother to get her hair cut and sit on the chair with the hair dryer reaching out above me like a giant helmet while I searched the *McCall's* magazine for the Betsy McCall paper dolls. This was all good, but it wasn't like playing with a sister.

There were times when my mother ignored my pleas for a sibling as she was making her grocery list or figuring out the prisoners' food budget for the next month, but every once in a while, she would get a wistful look in her eye and pause and say, "Another child might be nice. I thought we were through having children, but we have this big house and a baby would be nice!" Then she'd move on to the laundry and vacuuming, but this motivated me to continue my quest.

The months went by. Gary and Jackie went off to school each day, and I filled my days, but as soon as they got home, I'd rush to meet them and hear about their day. They did homework, read books, played games, and had friends and even birthday parties. They told me about having milk for their snack at school and on Fridays, it was chocolate. They had a desk, with a little chair and a pencil box filled with an eraser, a small box of crayons, and pencils. Gary had wooden puzzles in his classroom.

Before I knew it, Anne gave birth to a healthy son named Chuckie. My favorite days were when she would bring him over to our house and I could sit and hold him.

One day, as my mother was getting Anne some coffee, I heard her say, "I'm pregnant!"

I almost fell off the couch with poor bewildered Chuckie with me.

She continued, "Yes, I'm due in early July. We just decided we wanted another child. Maybe it was Gong's constant pestering, but we are very happy about another baby."

As Mom and Anne talked about baby things, I touched Chuckie's smooth skin and told him about my new sister. He would love her and they would have great times together. Now someone would give my mother a shower, and my sister would get a lot of presents. This was a red-letter day. I couldn't have been happier.

On a warm morning in July, I awoke, and my parents' bed across the room was empty and unmade. As I was slowly waking up, my dad came into the room to tell me that I had a baby brother. I was silent and in shock. Having a new baby was terrific, but what happened to my sister? We already had two boys.

"Kathleen, you know that a baby can be a girl or a boy, and our baby is your brother and we named him Mark."

I had to really think about this.

When my dad brought my mother and Mark home, we were all thrilled. Jackie, Gary, and I stood in awe as we examined our brother. He had dark eyes, dark hair, perfect white skin, and a sweet little mouth. I fell in love instantly. He was really something!

Kathleen and Jackie holding Mark, 1952.

With Mark's birth, my life changed in several ways. My mother taught me how to help bathe him and put baby crème on him. He smelled so sweet, and I could dress him and cuddle him. I could be a real help to her as she got through her postpartum days, and woke up nights to a crying and hungry child. Mother would tell the story that shortly after Mark was born, she needed to walk to the grocery store to pick up a few items. Mark was sleeping and I was watching him as he quietly slumbered in his bed. Remember that Dad was working in his office just on the other side of the wall. Mom left me in charge and went to the store, about three blocks from our house. As she gathered the items she needed, several people asked where the baby was. When Mother explained that she left him at home with Gong, they looked at her like she was an unfit parent.

"Certainly, you don't mean that Gong is in charge! Isn't she five?"

Mother was incredulous: "Of course, Gong is in charge. She can take care of him while I'm away for a few minutes."

I watched Mark like a hawk while Mother was gone. Although there were times when I wanted my mother to just sit down and play cards with me or read to me, Mark became my favorite project.

Two months after Mark's birth, the folks decided that we would take a relaxing trip to the Black Hills in South Dakota. True, a change of scenery is always nice, and this would allow them to be away from Dad's sheriff duties and Mom's chef duties for the prisoners for a while, but relaxing didn't seem to be in the cards. Taking a two-month-old baby, a five-year-old, a six-year-old, and a nine-year-old on a road trip was maybe not what the doctor ordered.

We had driven to Portland, Oregon, a couple of years earlier to visit Dad's brother Harry and his wife Elsie. Trips were few and far between, so this was a big deal. Along with the joys of the new baby, Mom was now tired from Mark's night-and-day feeding schedule. She had put up with the three of us all summer, and school would start soon. Dad asked Deputy Ernie to take over the helm for a few days and we prepared for a Labor Day trip to Mount Rushmore.

Mom borrowed a baby car bed from a friend and the royal blue rectangle was placed next to the back-seat door behind Mom. Mom also purchased a bottle warmer that was the latest technology. It was made of a blue-and-pink plastic material that plugged into the car cigarette lighter. Jackie, Gary, and I would take turns sitting in the front seat between Mom and Dad as our tan Ford cruised south. Obviously, when Mother had Mark in the front seat with her, we were all in the back seat pushing and shoving and doing the usual kid stuff—fighting over who got to sit by the door or whose arm crossed the imaginary line first.

Then there were the constant questions, "Are we there yet?"

When there was a need for calm, Mom would start singing:

> Show me the way to go home
> I'm tired and I want to go to bed
> I had a little drink about an hour ago

> And it went straight to my head
> Wherever I may roam
> Over land or sea or foam.

Then we were soothed and would relax, look out the window, maybe even take a nap. Now that I think about it, that was an odd song to sing to young kids, but it was very soothing and we sang along, forgetting our troubles for a while.

When we got to the Black Hills we saw the huge presidential heads on Mount Rushmore. Before Mom was married, she and some friends drove there while it was being built, so this was a favorite place of hers. Now we all stood and marveled at the magnificent sculpture on the mountain, and we all had a moment of inspiration and awe. Right in front of our eyes were Thomas Jefferson, George Washington, Abraham Lincoln, and Teddy Roosevelt. I had no clue who these men were, but seeing their huge faces carved into the mountain was simply amazing. Mom and Dad agreed. Seeing this incredible accomplishment made the hours in the car worthwhile.

Enjoying a South Dakota view. Gary, Jackie, Kathleen, and Mom.

The next morning we continued our journey, and soon Mark was hungry and started crying. Mom picked him up, got a bottle of formula from an insulated bag, and put it in the bottle warmer. I happened to be sitting by the door in the back seat looking out the window. Suddenly something smelled hot and Gary yelled "Fire!" as smoked drifted up from the bottle warmer. Fire really scared me. I immediately went into panic mode as my mind raced and I concluded that we were all going to burn to death in our car. I reached for the door handle to escape certain death. It was a good idea, but perhaps not while Dad was driving down the road.

So, let's review the situation: Mark is hungry and crying in the front seat, smoke and the smell of burning plastic is filling the car, and a five-year-old in the back seat has opened the door and is ready to jump. Home never looked so good.

Dad yelled, "Close the door, Kathleen! Jesus Christ! What are you thinking?"

Jackie pulled me back into the car, Mom unplugged the faulty bottle warmer, and hungry Mark screamed on. Dad must have been wondering which bag his ulcer medicine was packed in, while Mom gave Mark a partially warmed bottle of milk that silenced him and we all slowly caught our breath.

My heart pounded as Dad stopped the car and sternly told me that when the car was moving, you *DO NOT* open the door under any circumstances. Of course, seat belts hadn't been invented yet, so that was a pretty dangerous thing to do. My reaction had been an automatic reflex to flee from the smoke, but I realized that I needed to rethink my automatic reactions in the future. So, with the lingering scent of burned plastic, Mother cuddled the now contented Mark as he sucked down the last of the milk. The doors were all closed and I sobbed quietly as we journeyed on.

That afternoon we stopped at a huge Quonset building. I had never seen a swimming pool, and inside this mammoth building with a very high ceiling was this immense pool of water. Dad and the three of us kids put on our bathing suits, eager to leave the warm South Dakota afternoon behind as we entered the building with the strong smell of chlorine in the air, the fit lifeguard in a tall chair observing it all, and the happy sounds of kids jumping off the diving board, splashing in the pool, and generally having a great time.

Mom followed us, holding Mark, and she sat on a bench next to the wall, where she could watch us frolic in the water. Dad gave us firm instructions to stay close to each other and stay in the shallow area and then he left us as he swam several laps. The frustrations of the day left him and he mellowed in the cool, refreshing water.

Mom was watching us splash each other and attempt to swim. Dad came back and played with us and helped us all learn the "deadman's float" by having us lay on his hands flat on our backs in the water and telling us that if we relaxed we could float. The boys were both much better at this than I was. The relaxed part didn't work for me, so I was happy to hang onto the side of the pool and move a few feet forward and back. Mount Rushmore was terrific, but this swimming experience in the huge pool was truly the high point of our trip.

We got out of the pool, got back into our clothes, and were in the car ready to resume the trip when we heard Mom crying. This really got our attention. Mom didn't cry often. Through gulps of air and sobs, Mom reminded Dad that she didn't get to swim. While this trip was called a vacation, she continued to take care of their young baby, had to deal with kids jumping out of the car, bottle warmers burning up, the summer heat with no relief, and she had just had it.

The car was silent as we all focused on Mom and Dad. I was ashamed that I had tried to open the car door, and now Mom was crying. The boys and I sat very quietly, the refreshing time in the pool and the excitement of the past hour now forgotten as we saw our mother crying. I felt guilty that I had such a good time, and Mom, who loved to swim, just held the baby.

Dad instantly realized that he had enjoyed himself at Mom's expense and quickly said that we would all go back to the pool. Dad would hold Mark. We three kids would sit on the bench, and Mom could go swimming.

Mom put on her faded red bathing suit and we did just as Dad said. Sitting on the bench, we watched Mom enter the pool at the shallow end, splashing water on her upper body and slowly stooping into the water as she began swimming to the deep end. She swam several lengths, allowing the stress of the day to leave her body as she moved smoothly and rhythmically through the water. Even with the noise of active children enjoying the pool, Mom was in her own little world, temporarily away from us as the water soothed her tired body and frazzled nerves.

We kept our eyes on Mom, looking for a sign that she was feeling better. As she returned to the shallow end near us, she looked up and smiled. Our normal Mom was coming back to us. With that, we could all relax. Mom swam for a few more laps and then got out of the pool, an invigorated, new person.

We returned to the car and continued the trip home. The car was once again a calm and happy place. All of us in the back seat leaned back and relaxed as the soothing sounds of Mom's voice singing "Show me the way to go home, I'm tired and I want to go to bed…" filled the little tan car while we motored down the road.

Kathleen, Gary, Jackie and Mom holding Mark in South Dakota.

10.

My Brothers, My Buddies

Rolla, North Dakota
1952

"Siblings: A combination of a best friend and a pain in the neck. They might be the most annoying people around, but you still love them endlessly." —Anonymous

Halloween was coming. The days were getting shorter and winter was definitely on its way. My mother and I walked to the SuperValu, my mother pushing Mark in the pram. The wind was blowing and I was happy to have my winter parka on. There had been some snow, but the sidewalk was clear, so we could still use the baby buggy.

The store had several arched-back black cats and smiling bright orange jack-o'-lantern posters in the window. Orange-and-black candy corn was prominently displayed. My mother bought some sugar and flour to make trick-or-treat cookies and some apples for trick-or-treaters. I had never been trick-or-treating, but Mom said I could go this year.

"On Saturday, when the boys are home, we can go to Byrdie's and each of you can get a mask," Mom said as we walked the two blocks home carrying our groceries.

Wow! This would be fun.

"Do you just knock on the door and say 'Trick or treat'?" I asked.

"Yes, and when people give you candy, what do you say?"

I knew this one. "You say 'Thank you'!"

"Yes, and you must remember to do that!"

I was thoughtful for a minute and then asked, "What does 'trick or treat' mean?"

"It's an old saying. It means if you don't give me some candy, I'll trick you somehow."

"Like what?"

"Well, like soaping your windows. If someone doesn't give out candy, some older kids might take bars of soap and rub them on the windows of a house, and this leaves streaks and then the person that lives in the house has to wash their windows. You don't need to trick anyone, though. If a house has a porch light on, you can trick-or-treat there. It means they have treats to give children. If the porch light is off, you just go to the next house."

I couldn't wait. Halloween was going to be the best day ever. On Saturday, we all walked to Byrdie's. The sun was trying to come out, but dark clouds filled the sky. Byrdie's store was our favorite. It was actually the dime store and then the name changed to Ben Franklin, but no matter what they called it, it was the same store, and Mom's friend Byrdie Mongeon owned it.

Her store had everything: school supplies, comic books, stuff for the garden, dishes, hankies, and toys. I would walk down each aisle looking at all the treasures. There were more Halloween posters in the store and then a display table with masks. The boys and I looked at each one carefully. They had a red devil mask, a big bad wolf mask, a witch mask, scary ghost masks, skeleton masks, hobo masks, black cat masks. They were all made of rubber.

Jackie said, "All of these masks stick to your face after you wear them for a while and they are very hot."

Then I saw it. At the bottom of the scary ghost pile, there was a Casper the Friendly Ghost mask! That was it! That's the one I wanted. The boys picked their masks, too. On the walk home my mother reminded us how lucky we were. During the war, sugar was rationed and there was no candy available during those years.

October 31, 1952, was a Friday. As usual, Mom and I were home taking care of Mark. At breakfast, both boys were excited about Halloween treats at school that day.

"I get to go trick-or-treating," I said.

"Oh, no! said Jackie. "She will really slow us down. We can get twice as much candy if Gong doesn't go with us."

Mom was calm but firm as she said, "No, you need to take her. Gong gets to go this year, and you and Gary need to take care of her."

I was loving this. Both Jackie and Gary sighed and tried once again. "We could bring her candy," chimed in Gary, "Jackie's right. We want to go fast and she's slow."

"She's going!" Mom stated firmly and the discussion was over.

Both Jackie and Gary showed their disappointment and glared at me as Mom cleared the table. I couldn't help it. I smiled!

A month earlier, on September 29, my dad heard on the radio that President Truman was traveling across North Dakota on a train, making stops along the way and giving speeches supporting the Democratic candidate for President, Adlai Stevenson. One of the stops was Devils Lake, a town about 75 miles from Rolla. The president would speak from the rear platform of his railroad car. He would be in Devils Lake at about 2:30, and a few minutes after his speech, he would be leaving for the next stop.

Like most North Dakotans, my parents voted Republican. But since FDR's programs had helped so many farmers during the depression, my mother was a true fan of

Roosevelt. Political party aside, how often did a president of the United States travel this close to Rolla?

Even though it was a Monday, my dad decided he and the boys would go to see President Truman. As soon as I heard about it, I wanted to join in on the fun. I knew we had seen presidents' faces at Mount Rushmore, so I knew they were very important. Sometimes we heard President Truman talk on the radio, so even though I wasn't sure what they did, I wanted to go see one, too. My dad quickly nixed that idea, and so the boys and my dad went off to see the president while my mother and I took care of Mark and fed the prisoners.

Trick-or-treating was another story! I was going to do that. There was some kind of justice in the world.

On Halloween night, we ate a quick dinner and then got dressed in our parkas and our prized masks. Mom gave us each a pillowcase to put our candy in and we were off. We ran past the courthouse next door and then stopped at each house that had a light on. It was so much fun!

By the time I got to a porch, Jackie and Gary were moving on to the next one, but my bag was filling up. There were lots of small groups of kids on the streets. Each group seemed to be guiding a smaller child along, too. There were no parents. Just kids out having fun. A few times the boys slowed down and yelled for me to hurry up. I was trying.

It didn't take long for us to circle back around toward home. It was getting colder and it was very dark. As we ran down the sidewalk by a vacant lot, three big boys came charging down the street running toward us. Jackie yelled, "Hurry up, Gong!"

Following Jackie's lead, I started running as fast as I could. One of the big boys quickly grabbed my bag and pushed me down. I yelled for my brothers and began crying as I tried to get the dirt off my face. I had taken my mask off shortly after we started out because Jackie was right, my face was sweaty. My mask was hanging by the thin elastic headband from my wrist. Jack and Gary heard my cry, and they quickly came back as the big boys ran in the other direction. I had fallen on my face. My knee was scraped, but worst of all, my bag of treats was gone.

"They took my candy!" I sobbed.

We were just a couple of blocks from home, so the boys helped me brush off my jacket and said they would both share their candy with me. We slowly walked home.

Mom was at the door giving out cookies when we arrived. Jackie told her what happened and she said, "Oh Lumpy, come in!" Lumpy was my mother's shortened version of "Little lump of Love." She took me in, washed my face, and got the bottle of Mercurochrome for my scraped knee under my torn corduroy pants.

My brothers were sorting out their treats. There were several wax paper-wrapped popcorn balls, pumpkin-shaped sugar cookies, apples, Tootsie Rolls, pieces of Dubble Bubble bubblegum, jelly beans, pennies and nickels, and green and red suckers. My brothers went through their stash and created a third pile of treats for me. I had the best brothers in the whole world! They were sharing with me and I felt like a queen. A queen without a Casper mask, however. When I fell, I guess the mask fell off my arm, so it was gone, too.

Trick-or-treating was a lot harder than I thought it would be. But I remembered the mothers that gave us treats at each door and the way my brothers shared with me. Next year I would be six and I could run faster, so maybe I wouldn't lose my treat bag. Most kids were nice, but some were just plain bad.

11.

May the Force be with You

Rolla, North Dakota
1952

"Everything is hard before it is easy." —Goethe

I grabbed my parka off the hook and tried to put it on, but the zipper was stuck. I walked to Dad's office door and listened. It was quiet, so I cautiously opened the door and saw Ernie sitting at the desk.

"Well, hello, Kathleen." he said.

"Hi, Ernie. Could you help me? My zipper's stuck."

"Come here."

I walked over to Ernie, who wiggled the zipper and freed a path for it to close.

"Thanks, Ernie."

"Where are you going?"

"Outside to play. The sun's out and I want to build a snow fort."

I made an outline in the snow and then made some snow blocks to create a wall. When the boys came home we all worked on creating a fort until we were too cold to continue. Inside, we could smell onions frying. Mom was preparing dinner. Dad was sitting at the table running his hand through his thinning hair. There was no smile for us, only a frown, and it seemed like he didn't even see us. We walked toward him, but his mind was elsewhere. What was going on?

The *Turtle Mountain Star* was on the table, and right on the front page was a picture of a man that looked like a nice Grandpa. I looked at the picture and asked, "Who is this?"

Dad's distant stare left his face as he suddenly saw me. He cleared his throat and looked at the newspaper and sighed.

"We have a new president," he said. "President Eisenhower was elected yesterday. We also had our election here and I lost. There will be a new sheriff. I won't be sheriff anymore."

Suddenly the room was silent. We all stared at Dad as our ice-crusted mittens and snow-covered jackets began to drip on the floor.

"What will we do?" Jackie asked.

Dad thought for a minute and said, "We'll figure it out. Hang up your jackets. Mom will have dinner ready soon."

Turtle Mountain Star, November 6, 1952.

Election day had come and gone, and even though Dad and I had spent some time driving around the county delivering pamphlets and shaking hands, the votes were counted and his defeat was clear. In two months, he wouldn't have a job and we wouldn't have a house to live in.

This setback was a total shock to the folks. Mom and Dad were both well respected in town. In fact, Dad won in Rolla, 224 votes to his opponent's 51, but total votes from the county had him losing. It seemed that most people were pretty apathetic about the election, maybe assuming Dad would win. He lost to a man who was rumored to have provided alcohol to the Indians. The folks did not analyze the situation long because in two months we had to move and Dad needed to have a new job.

Suddenly the joys of living in our beloved sheriff's house had a real temporary feeling. The future was beginning to look scary, as Mom and Dad tried to figure out their next move. Dad's ulcer flared up and he lost his appetite.

Since her early childhood years, my mother had experienced "sick headaches." She was the nervous child in her family, and her anxiety often led to debilitating migraine headaches. They would usually start with "flashing lights," which she explained were zigzag colored lines of light blurring her vision. These episodes usually lasted about twenty minutes, but they were a precursor to a pounding headache that followed and sent her to bed for at least a day, sometimes two.

After the initial shock, reality set in and the folks considered their options. Rolla was a town that supported area farmers. We didn't have a farm to go to, so what could Dad do in town? His passion was always photography and he was skilled in that field. It just didn't provide a living to support six people.

There was a vacant store at the end of Main Street. Upstairs, the building had two rented apartments in the front and a larger one-bedroom vacant apartment in the rear. After growing up on a farm, Dad was handy with tools, and if he made some changes to the store and the apartment, it might work for us.

Mom could contribute her college accounting skills. They could open a clothing store. Dad could also set up a darkroom with the equipment he already had on part of the store's mezzanine. He could create a small studio in the back room of the store to take children's pictures. Maybe he could also take school pictures and develop and sell them.

On December 18, 1952, the *Turtle Mountain Star* ran the following:

> Maurice J. Holstad, whose term as Sheriff of Rolette County is expiring at the end of the year plans to enter business in Rolla. Mr. Holstad is not yet ready to announce the type of business he will operate, but said he is considering several possibilities.

There were downsides to this plan. One was the store's location. There were four other clothing stores in town, and this building was near the edge of town. On a day with normal temperatures, a walk to the edge of town would be enjoyable, but on a fifty-below-zero winter day, walking an extra couple of blocks with the frozen prairie wind in your face would make you stop at a more centrally located store for basic clothing items. Also, the one-bedroom apartment was a small space for all of us. In time, maybe my parents could save money and buy a house in town.

Gamble-Skogmo Inc. was a conglomerate of retail chains selling hardware, appliances, furniture, groceries, auto accessories, clothing, etc. By 1939, according to *Prairie Business* magazine, Gamble-Skogmo had 1,700 stores in the United States. It was headquartered in Minnesota.

At Dad's request, representatives from Skogmos arrived in town wearing their business suits and fedoras and met with my parents. The folks made the decision to start a Skogmos clothing store. We began packing our things and preparing for the move to downtown. Mom lifted the lid on our Norwegian trunk and packed some of her most treasured items. I was thrilled. Living on Main Street would be exciting!

With the sting of the election defeat behind us, we were on a roll. We were embarking on an adventure and a new challenge. The unspoken sentiment, but the newfound knowledge, was that if this didn't work out, we would have to move to an area that provided my father more work opportunities. Both folks loved the Rolla community and their friends and activities. Leaving my mother's family, who lived close by, seemed unthinkable. Our grandparents, aunts, uncles, and cousins were a huge part of our life. Mom and Dad were highly motivated to make this work.

Main Street in Rolla. Our store was the third building on the right.

Our store and new home was just a few blocks from the sheriff's house. We were moving to a two-story brick building that had a vacant store with a high ceiling on the first floor and three apartments on the second floor. About twenty-five steep stairs attached to the outside wall of our store led up to the apartments. I was intimidated by the height of the stairs; a fall would really hurt. Mom could only think about carrying groceries up those stairs. There was a small landing at the top of the stairs. Entering and going to the left took you down the hall to the two front apartments and the bathroom. Turning right at the entrance led to the front door of our apartment.

The two apartments at the front of the building had one bedroom each, plus a small galley kitchen with a nook and a built-in table. Each apartment also had a living room dominated by a large brown oil burner, with a stovepipe connecting to the chimney.

Two sisters in their mid-twenties, Mavis and June Nurmi, worked at the bank and lived in the first apartment. Mrs. Galloway lived in the second front apartment. She was a grandmother, and I was thrilled to have a potential friend in the same building.

The only bathroom on this floor was at the end of the hall. We would all share it. The bathroom had a toilet, sink, and shower. A small index card on the wall indicated which days each apartment was allowed to shower. My dad was the new landlord, and our family's shower days would be Wednesday and Saturday. For bathing on other days, my mother would wheel in the washtub from the laundry room. At night, we had a bucket with a magazine on top for anyone that needed a toilet in a hurry.

We were moving into the rear apartment, which was the largest but still very small compared to the sheriff's house. The front door opened into an area with hooks on the wall to hang coats and remove boots. The square metal oil burner, which took up a corner of the living room, heated the apartment.

Our apartment also had one bedroom, but the overall size of this apartment was about double the size of the others. Before we moved in, Dad created a small bedroom for Jackie and Gary by partitioning off part of the living room. He attached sheetrock to a wooden frame between the kitchen wall and the front door creating a space large enough for the boys' bunk beds. This left a very small living area that included our dining table and a chest of drawers in which we kept the family clothes. Right behind the table was a window that looked out onto the black tar paper roof of Hagen's grocery store next door.

The Hagens were very kid-friendly, and we would often run next door to pick up something Mom needed for dinner. Mom hung the drapes from the sheriff's house on this window and got a new oil cloth for the table, making our decorating complete.

The tiny kitchen was just beyond the table. Our Gibson refrigerator fit there. The sink, drainboard, and a short counter occupied the end of the kitchen. On the opposite wall, the small four-burner apartment-sized stove completed the kitchen. The living room area across from the boys' new bedroom had room for a couch with a lamp at either end and our Crosley console radio.

Mom and Dad's bed was placed in one corner of their bedroom, and opposite their bed was a bunk bed for Mark and me. Mark had the bottom bunk. I was thrilled with the top bunk. Dad attached a plywood board about one-third the length of the bed so I wouldn't fall out. Mom's vanity with the 1940s circle mirror stood next to our bunk beds. Just outside the bedroom at the rear of the apartment was a laundry area. Wooden indoor steps went down to the store or an outside door.

The quarters were tight, but no one seemed fazed by the closeness. Gone were the pretty woodwork and the feeling of spaciousness we had enjoyed in the sheriff's house. In its place, however, were nice neighbors right down the hall, the challenge of climbing the outdoor stairs, and the thrill of living on Main Street.

We had no yard, so Dad installed wire fencing to define a small play area for us behind the store. We had a sandbox, but most of all, this little cage was a safe area separating me and Mark from any cars driving down the back alley. It was convenient for Dad and Mom to work downstairs in the store and then walk right up to the apartment on the enclosed back stairs without having to deal with North Dakota weather when it was cold and stormy.

The stores in Rolla were all closed on Sundays and opened 9 to 5 or 6 on other days. The busiest day for us was Saturday, when the store was open until 9 PM, as that was when area farmers came into town to get supplies and socialize. Mother hired Mrs. Lavager, an Indian woman from the reservation, to come in and take care of Mark when she was needed in the store.

True to his vision, Dad set up a darkroom and a small photo studio in the back of the store. By saving $25 worth of yellow receipts from our store, customers could get a black-and-white 8" x 10" photo of their child for a dollar. Dad hung a copy of each child's photo at the top of the fixtures in the store, so in time the store was surrounded with the smiling faces of most of the children in town. He also contracted with the Rolla school to take the school photographs each year.

The photo advertisement for the store, starring Mark.

I loved the store. Remodeling was completed and fixtures were delivered. A couple of men in suits from Gamble-Skogmo helped Mom and Dad with store setup. Soon huge boxes of something they called inventory began arriving. I couldn't wait to see what was inside. As it turned out, it was shoes, dresses, baby clothes, men's work shirts, bib overalls, and towels.

The smell of the new merchandise filled the store. As the store was being set up, we ran around the fixtures, finding new places to hide and enjoying the excitement of the store opening. Mom and Dad were both very busy marking all the "inventory" with price tags. Some items were going to be on sale to entice the whole town to come to the grand opening on Monday, March 30, at 10 AM. Free coffee and cookies would be served until 3 PM. This was a party. "Grand Opening" and "Sale" signs hung from the ceiling of the store. Dad bought a full-page advertisement from the *Turtle Mountain Star.*

> It is with the feeling of pardonable pride that we are announcing the opening of our new store—The Skogmos Store.
>
> WE ARE READY! The long weeks remodeling and preparation are over and it is with feeling of pride that we present our new ultra modern store to the public. Everything is ready for your inspection and approval. Our quality merchandise at our ever-so reasonable prices offer you really marvelous values and we give you our pledge to offer you the best merchandise—at prices you'll be glad to pay—and render the best service and satisfaction to all our friends and most valued customers. You are always welcome at our store! Make Skogmos your headquarters.
>
> Maurice and Lyda Holstad

Sale prices included:

- Lovely House Dresses that will wash like hankies and stay everlastingly fresh. $2.98
- Men's Hi-Grade Sport Shirts all the new styles and colors-$2.98
- Men's Hi-Quality work shoes-$7.50
- SPECIAL! Ladies Regular 49c Rib-To-Toe

- Anklets-39c
- INFANT FINEST BLANKETS 6-inch Satin binding-crib size-$3.49
- Regular 49c BATH TOWELS Sizes 20 X 40-in. Assorted colors. A great value at 33c.

Since Saturday was the big shopping day in town, it is curious that the folks chose to have their Grand Opening on a Monday. They were having a special drawing for a door prize that would be given away Saturday night at 8 PM. Maybe they believed that curiosity about a new store in a little town that rarely had much change would be enough to pull in the Saturday crowds. Also, it may have been to save costs by offering the coffee and cookies on a slow Monday.

The opening of our Skogmos, featuring the men in fedoras from Minneapolis.

The remodeling was complete and Skogmos was ready for business.

Once the folks bought the store, it kept them busy and their time for social activities diminished. They traded off working in the store during the week. There were orders to prepare; bills to pay; and inventory to unpack, mark, and shelve. Displays needed to be changed in the front windows, seasonal banners needed to be put up, banking had to be done daily.

Since I was still not in school when the store opened, my job was to do the banking. Dad would count the money, fill out the deposit slip, and put the money in a canvas bank bag for me to take to the bank, which was one block down the street. The bank was a large, imposing building, at least to my five-year-old eyes. I basked in the glow of responsibility as I carried the day's receipts into the bank and waited for my turn to hand the bag to the friendly bank teller. The bank was polished and impressive, and all the employees were conscientious and professional. It had almost the same feeling as going into church. You just knew you had to be quiet and on your best behavior. This was a very serious time for me each day.

When I got home with the change Dad needed for the day and the receipt for the deposit, I was met with a smile from Dad. The boys were in school, Mom was taking care of the baby, and Dad and I were running the store. It didn't get much better than this.

There was nothing dull about living on Main Street! From the very beginning, the daily activity of Rolla intrigued me. I could help unpack new merchandise, take my dolls on a tour of the store and decide what items to purchase from the baby department. I could look at all the dresses and shoes. I enjoyed being in the store with my father. Customers were fun to watch, and my mother was happy to have me down with Dad while she took care of Mark and kept the laundry and food preparation going.

My sixth birthday was approaching. Dad had to make a trip to the Gamble store in Rugby, about an hour and a half away, to pick up some merchandise and he told me I could have a doll buggy or a bicycle for my birthday present. The Gamble hardware store had both, so he just needed to know before he left. What a dilemma! I wanted them both. I had never had a doll buggy and I loved playing with my doll. With a doll buggy, I could give her rides up and down the street. A bike would also be fun, but I wasn't sure since I didn't know how to ride one. I decided that I would ask the boys for help in making the decision when they got home from school.

It didn't take any time at all for my brothers to decide what my birthday present should be. Who in their right mind would want a doll buggy? You must get the bike. We could ride all over town this summer. I raced to tell Dad the good news.

The next week, Dad came home with a shiny yellow-and-blue Hiawatha girl's bike. Both of the boys had their bikes, and we took my new prize to the parking area behind the store, where they took turns riding it. Just as I was beginning to think the doll buggy might have been a better choice, Dad came out and helped me onto the seat. He held the bike up as I pedaled and tried to get my balance. Soon he had to go back to work, so Jackie and Gary took over holding the bike and helping me balance as I struggled to keep myself upright.

By the end of the week, I had mastered it and my world immediately increased in size. We really could ride all over town. We went up and down streets in the residential area, way down to the fairgrounds. I couldn't keep up with the boys, as they were really fast bike riders, but I loved the wind in my face and the thrill of going down the sloping driveways and coasting down hills.

It was May and winter was over. Spring had the best weather. Life was very, very good just riding my new bike. The boys were right. I needed to continue following their advice!

Before I knew it school was out and the boys had the summer off. Main Street was bustling. I sat on the steps of the store and watched the cars and trucks slowly moving down the street. Sometimes cars would stop at the hotel across the street from us. If someone interesting stopped, I would run down and watch them get out of their cars.

The most exciting visitors to town were often from nearby Canada. I enjoyed listening to their strange pronunciation of words. Their vacation was called a "holiday" and "about" sounded like "aboot." I could usually spot them by their plaid shirts.

Mark was getting cuter every day. The boys and I were thrilled when he started talking. Living with Mark was our first experience with a baby, and we all enjoyed his development as he learned to move around the house by scooting on his bottom, never developing the traditional crawl on all fours. When he was learning to talk, we would encourage him and were all impressed when he learned some nursery rhymes. I can still hear him reciting: "Humpy, Dumpy sat on the wall..." His pronunciation was almost correct, and he would stand on a chair in his red or green overalls and his Rudy Kazooty sweatshirt as we applauded him. Dad borrowed a machine that recorded sound on a record from Toivo Valiki's electronics store and we could listen to Mark on a record. We had confidence that Mark would soon pronounce Humpty Dumpty correctly because he was certainly the smartest little boy in town.

Mark

Our store was next to the green and white City Services gas station. On the other side of the station was a furniture store and next to that was the John Deere Implement Store. About midsummer, Mr. and Mrs. Balwig bought the furniture store. They moved above their store just like we did. They had three daughters. Sharon was my age and Arlene was younger. They also had a baby. It was great having someone to play with. I quickly introduced myself, and we became inseparable.

We went into their store and picked out our favorite furniture and then on to our store and shopped for clothing for our pretend families. Some days we borrowed some of Mark's receiving blankets and bobby pinned them to our hair. We'd put our dolls in our wagon and run up and down Main Street, pretending we were Sister Bertha. Occasionally we would set up a Kool-Aid stand at the corner of our block nearest the theater and sell cool drinks to customers attending the movies.

Sometimes the high school band would march down the street on a warm Saturday night. We would run down toward the center of town to get a good view of the students practicing their songs for the football games when school started. A John Philip Sousa march would start, and the performers would get into formation and march back to school.

There was so much to entertain me that summer, and my next adventure was starting school. I couldn't wait to learn to read.

12.

Let the School Bells Ring

Rolla, North Dakota
1953-1954

"Siblings will take different paths and life may separate them, but they will forever be bonded by having begun their journey in the same boat." —Anonymous

Before I knew it, my mother was turning the calendar and up popped September. I had been waiting two years for this month. At last, I got to go to school.

One evening a month earlier as I was getting ready for bed, my dad asked, "Are you ready to go to school, Kathleen?"

"I really want to go to school," I said, "but I'm afraid that I might suck my thumb and everyone will think I'm a baby."

I was still sucking my thumb at night, but I wanted to grow up.

"Well, let's work on breaking that habit," Dad said.

"I've tried, but whenever I'm tired and in bed, my thumb just goes up into my mouth."

Dad thought a moment and then said, "If you really want to quit we can try something."

He walked out the door and downstairs to the store. A few minutes later he returned with two small brown bags and some string.

"Put your pajamas on and get ready for bed and then I'll fix your hands."

I quickly prepared for bed and came back, eager to see what the next step was. He tied a brown sack around each hand and sent me to bed. It felt strange lying in bed with my hands in bags. When I could no longer stay awake I closed my eyes and my hand moved toward my face as usual. The bag touched my face and my favorite thumb could not come out. I rolled over and went to sleep. Dad continued this procedure for about four days until I was content to sleep without a thumb in my mouth. Now I could focus on school.

Preparation for school began with a trip to Byrdie's dime store to buy school supplies. First of all, I needed a pencil box. There were several different sizes and prices. Some had two layers, and the bottom layer had a drawer you could pull open. Some were small and only had room for about four pencils.

Mother said I didn't have to get the smallest one, but I certainly didn't need the largest one either. I picked one that was red and had room for about three pencils. I got a Chief pencil tablet that had a red Indian on the cover.

Next, she chose a box of pencils that we would all share, and we each got a box of crayons. Some boxes had 8 crayons, some 16, some 24, and the big one had 48 crayons. Once again, we didn't need the smallest, but 16 crayons were certainly enough for any child.

My mother was buying supplies for all of us. My brothers had better things to do than shop for school stuff.

First day of school. Jackie, Kathleen, and Gary.

The first day of school dawned clear and cool. We got our bikes and Dad took a picture of us in front of the store. We were ready for the challenges of the new year. I was starting first grade, Gary was a third grader, and Jackie was in the sixth grade.

I parked my bike in the rack at the side of the school and walked toward the entrance of the two-story brick building. It was like a massive fort or castle. I had been in it before, visiting my brothers' classrooms with my mother, but today I was a student.

I joined the rush of children entering through the giant doors and looking for their classrooms. The stairs to the left went to the higher grades, but I knew that Miss Bateson's first-grade classroom was down the hall and to the right, last door on the left.

I was silent as I listened to older students greeting their friends and laughing and talking. The school had that institutional smell of floor wax and textbooks. The high ceilings inside the building made me feel very insignificant, but I had arrived. I was with the "big kids." No more staying at home. My stomach was filled with butterflies.

Rolla School.

"A good education can change anyone. A good teacher can change everything." —Anonymous

Miss Bateson seemed about a hundred years old. She had taught Jackie and Gary and every first grader in town. She wore thick, beige cotton stockings and braided her dark hair, pinning the braids to the top of her head. She was a no-nonsense person and had no problem controlling a class of over thirty of us. I loved our little desks and the small red chairs in a half circle ready for reading. The worksheets were exciting. The wooden puzzles were a treat for completing work early. Recess was a thrill, as I found friends I knew:

Carolyn, Beverly, and Lois. I also met new kids from the country that came to school each day on the bus.

Miss Bateson's first-grade class.

All too soon, the weather changed and winter came. Now in addition to spending ten minutes each morning getting dressed to leave home, we arrived at school and spent a large portion of each day undressing, dressing for recess, undressing and dressing for lunch play, undressing again, and finally dressing once more to go home.

We stood by the hot radiators, sending steam into the room as we took off our boots, often fumbling with stubborn buckles. Then off came the mittens, the scarf around the neck, the parka, the snow pants, and the cardigan sweater.

The rooms often felt like a sauna. We hung all of these items on hooks near the door, feeling liberated, as we could suddenly move freely—that is, until it was time for recess and the process began in reverse. The classroom always had a smell of damp clothes roasting as we struggled to understand phonics and read about the adventures of Dick, Jane, Sally, and Puff.

During these thrilling school days, my mother was home caring for Mark and helping Dad in the store. She was feeling abnormally tired and would fall asleep each day when she put Mark down for his nap. She finally went to the doctor, who told her she was pregnant. Mother's first reaction was concern. We were all in the apartment waiting for dinner that night when Dad came up the back stairs and Mother made her announcement.

"I'm pregnant!" she stammered.

We were all surprised, but she and Dad were shocked.

"I'll be almost forty-one when I have this baby. You'll be forty-five," Mother said with tears welling in her eyes and running down her face. "That is too old to be having children. How can we handle five children?"

Dad came over and hugged her and said, "It will be fine. We'll work it out."

Mother wasn't sure. "We're so crowded already. How can we fit a baby into this apartment?"

"We'll put the crib in our room," Dad said.

Mother groaned and said, "We already have Gong and Mark in our room. How much can one room take?"

Dad gave Mom a hug. "I'll start dinner," he said.

Four pairs of eyes followed him as he opened the refrigerator and began taking out eggs and bacon. We were all uneasy as we looked around the apartment. Where would we put a baby? Then it hit me. This could be my sister. Wow! We would make room. This is the best news yet.

Miss Bateson distributed a box of musical instruments to our class. We were going to have a rhythm band, whatever that was. Some kids had drums, some had triangles, some had tambourines. I had wood blocks.

We were going to perform for our parents soon, so we practiced on our instruments each day. We also learned a few songs to sing. We marched around the classroom to music on the phonograph and sang each song many times. On the day of our performance, Miss Bateson gave us each a purple-and-gold (our school colors) satin cape to wear. We looked fabulous. We were professionals.

Dad tended the store so Mom could attend the production. That evening I heard the folks discussing the event.

"Guess whose voice was the loudest?"

Dad didn't have to say anything because he knew.

Mom continued with a smile on her face, "The enthusiasm was definitely there; if she could only carry a tune!"

I still remember overhearing this. I was so into the joy of singing that I had no idea my voice wasn't blending well, so to speak.

Years later my sons and then, a generation later, my grandsons would say, as I belted out a song, "Don't sing!" At first, especially with the second generation so precisely echoing the first, I thought they might have a hereditary hearing defect. But when my husband assured me it would be better for all if I didn't sing, I finally got the message.

I have since learned to stifle my urge to sing until I am driving alone in my car. Then I turn up the volume on the radio, sing as if the world were my stage, stomp on the gas, and blast onto the freeway.

The days became colder and snow was the norm as Christmas approached. One of our favorite family traditions was opening one present on Christmas Eve. Each year we got a couple of small presents, maybe some new slippers or pajamas, possibly a book or a game, and always an Avon gift. We went to great lengths to see that such presents were not our Christmas Eve choice.

Every town had at least one Avon representative and probably more. Mom would always take a minute and listen to whoever knocked on the door representing Avon. We had no TV, but the folks subscribed to the *Saturday Evening Post*, and either *Look* or *Life*. These kept Mom up-to-date with advertisements on the latest beauty products and, of course, the radio was constantly telling us to use Ivory Soap and Ipana Toothpaste. But to have another woman, usually someone she knew, stop by with the latest Avon catalog of products was reason for Mom to take a break, often make a cup of coffee for her guest, and look at the beauty creams and lipsticks.

At Christmas time, the catalog also featured children's soap cleverly packaged in a snowman box or shampoo in a Santa bottle. We always looked for the Avon gift with the wonderful smell under the small tree first. Usually the small size was a giveaway, but just to be sure we would sniff the packages because we definitely didn't want to open that one on Christmas Eve. Santa would bring us each one present on Christmas morning, and that gift was never wrapped.

We raided Dad's drawer for four socks to set under the tree, each with one of our names written on a piece of paper and taped on it. Then we put out the milk and cookies for Santa. With those tasks completed, we prepared for bed, always resolving that we would not sleep because we wanted to stay awake to see Santa.

Jackie and Gary were wise to the secrets of Christmas, but they went along with our shenanigans anyway. Mark and I went off to our bunk beds, and Jackie and Gary to their bunk beds adjacent to the living room. Mom and Dad quietly slipped out their bedroom door through the laundry room to the stairs and down to the store mezzanine. By this time, Mark and I were asleep, and Gary and Jackie were tossing and turning, too excited to sleep.

There was a heat register in the middle of the living room, and soon sounds from the store got the boys' attention. Boxes were being opened, things were being moved, something was placed on the floor, and they could hear Mom and Dad talking in hushed tones.

Jackie crawled out of bed, immediately missing his warm blankets. He crawled to the register and put his head close to the metal grid. He heard a "tap, tap, tap" and sat up with a smile on his face. Something big was going on down there. Could it be that there was a train in their future? Jackie and Gary had both wanted one.

There were Lionel train advertisements in the back of some comic books and Jackie's *Boys' Life*. That was a big present, and they really didn't think they would ever get one, but what else would require the folks to be so busy on Christmas Eve?

As soon as the thought had entered his head, Jackie turned and whispered to Gary, the breath from each word visible in the cold air, "Gary, get up! We're getting a train! Bring your blanket!"

In a flash, Gary jumped out of bed and crawled to Jackie dragging his blanket. "It is really cold," he said.

The two boys covered themselves and put their heads on the register as the "Tap! Tap! Tap!" continued.

"What's Dad doing?" Gary asked.

Jackie thought for a moment and said, "He must be fastening the track to a board so we can play with the train on the mezzanine."

"That must be it," said Gary. "We couldn't play with it up here. It would take up the whole living room floor and Mark would be walking into it. Then with the baby coming, there would be no room at all."

There were more muffled sounds coming from below and then the sound of an electric train on a track. Both boys smiled. Wow! They continued to listen as the train circled round and round the track. Periodically, the train sped up and then they heard a crash, as the locomotive and all the cars fell off the track. They could hear it being set up again and then off it went, again and again.

Gary finally said, "Is Dad putting it together or playing with it? It could be worn out by Christmas."

The next morning we got up to stockings filled with an apple and an orange in the toe, and a chocolate Santa or two. Then wrapping paper flew as we opened our gifts. I have no recollection of what I got that year because the Lionel electric train in the mezzanine for the boys was gift enough for all of us.

We took Mark down, and he loved watching the train circle the track. We all wanted to drive the train by moving the controller. The track was a rectangle with rounded corners, and at one end the track piece contained a switch that allowed the train to go into a figure 8 configuration in the middle.

One piece of track also had an uncoupler. A cord from the track was attached to a button you pushed to separate the cars. Jackie and Gary traded off running the train. I wanted to do it, too, but they convinced me I lacked the maturity for that task. It was really something boys did, but I could push the button on the uncoupler.

The gift also came with a small bottle of tiny white pills. Putting one of these in the train's smokestack made smoke puff from the locomotive as it whizzed around the track. It is difficult to find words to describe our excitement with the train. For years it would entertain us as we created villages and hauled Lincoln Logs, Tinkertoys, and small cars around and around that track.

At some point, Mother had me join the American Legion Junior Auxiliary. Dad was a member of the American Legion, a veteran's service organization that emphasizes patriotism, and in this small community, socialization. The Legion Hall was a log cabin in the middle of Rolla. I always thought of Abe Lincoln as I entered the building.

Mother was a member of the American Legion Auxiliary, so it was only fitting that I join the Junior Auxiliary. Several of my friends were members, and we saluted the flag, put wreaths on local veterans' graves on Memorial Day, and sold poppies as a fund-raiser. I looked forward to our meetings.

This year, we were preparing a play celebrating George Washington. On our meeting date close to his birthday, we were supposed to arrive with our costumes ready for our performance. My assigned role was Martha Washington.

In late February, Mother began slowing down. Her stomach was huge and she was having trouble sleeping. She started having labor pains and was admitted to the hospital. We all tried to help Dad as he ran the store and kept the home fires burning without Mom.

In the midst of it all, I needed a Martha Washington costume, so Dad and I looked in Mother's closet and found one of her skirts that almost touched the floor on me. Using one of Mark's diaper pins, we made the waist fit. Mark's yellow crocheted baby blanket from Aunt Elsie, worn over my school blouse, became my shawl. I was thrilled. Anyone could see that I was Martha Washington.

The next day, I left school with my costume in a grocery bag on my way to the Legion Hall. I walked right by the front of the hospital and stood across the street scanning the windows for any sign of my mother. Was she feeling all right? Did she have a new baby? Would she be home soon? I couldn't wait to have her home. I couldn't linger long, though, because our auxiliary meeting was about to begin.

As it turned out, Mother came home without a baby, and then a few days later her pains returned and Dad took her back to the hospital, this time coming home with Mom and our sister Nancy.

Yes, it was a girl. She was beautiful. Her small crib was placed in the center of the bedroom we shared with the folks and life went on. Thankfully, Nancy didn't put the folks through the trauma I did as a new baby.

My baby sister arrived. Kathleen and Nancy, 1954.

Mother always said, "God wouldn't give me a difficult child at this age."

Nancy was a joy for her and all of us. Very soon, we couldn't imagine life without her.

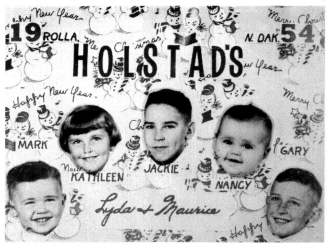

Our Christmas card in 1954.

13.

Small Town Living

Rolla, North Dakota
1954-1955

"A life is not important except in the impact it has on other lives." —Jackie Robinson

"Guess what, Sharon? We're getting a spin dryer." I said to my neighbor.

"What's a spin dryer?"

"It's very modern. We have a wringer that my mother turns by hand to get the water out of the clothes, and my dad said the spin dryer will help her a lot on wash day."

The laundry area just outside our apartment's bedroom briefly became an entertainment center for us as we gathered around the new, rapidly spinning machine. Previously, Mother had to put each piece of laundry through the wringer and then hang the damp clothes on racks on the landing at the top of the stairs.

The spin dryer was automatic. Put several pieces of clothing in the tub and press a button, and the clothes spun as the water was forced from them. Soon after we tired of watching this, Dad came home from Munro Hardware across the street with a mangle ironer. This machine was about the size of a desk, and the only place it would fit in our apartment was in the bedroom, right at the foot of Mom and Dad's bed. That left just enough room to walk beside our bunk bed.

Mother showed me how to iron on the mangle. This was before permanent press or drip-dry clothing that needed no ironing. Cotton clothing right off the drying racks or clotheslines was stiff and wrinkled.

The only option prior to our mangle was sprinkling the clothes so they would be slightly damp, then standing at an ironing board with a flatiron and pressing them. Now, I would sit down and pretend I was driving as I pressed my knee against the pedal and the hot roller was engaged, making wrinkled hankies, pillowcases, sheets, blouses, and men's shirts flat and smooth. We were suddenly a modern home.

Cars were changing rapidly, too. The basic look of the forties' models became flashy, with new designs and bright colors, dramatic fins, and pizzazz. By the end of the 1950s, one in six working Americans worked directly or indirectly for the auto industry. The United States became the world's largest automobile manufacturer.[1]

Each year my brothers and I eagerly anticipated the new car models. We all knew a 1953 Ford from a 1954, or the latest Chevy from last year's version.

Gary came into the apartment one day in the summer of 1954 and shouted, "Gong, you have to come to Wes Howson's with me. He's giving away car T-shirts!"

I was incredulous. "You mean we don't have to pay for them?"

"No! They're free!"

"Let's go!"

In a flash Gary and I were on our bikes, riding from the back of our store, past the creamery, and down the street to Howson's Ford dealership. We parked our bikes and looked through the large glass windows. Gary was right: Wes Howson was handing out T-shirts with the 1954 Ford Fairlane on them.

We cautiously opened the door and walked into his store. We became shy, unsure if we should be there.

"Hi, kids! Did you come for a shirt?" Wes greeted us.

"Yes, we did!"

---

1. https://en.wikipedia.org/wiki/American_automobile_industry_in_the_1950s

"Okay! Here is a Ford Fairlane shirt for you Gary and one for Kathleen."

This was unbelievable. We were admiring the shirts when more kids entered as word of these treasures quickly spread around town.

Gary and I got back on our bikes with shirts in hand and rode home to show the folks. When we entered the store, Dad was busy with a customer, but as soon as he was free we showed him our gifts.

He admired them with us and then said, "That was really nice of Wes. Did you thank him?"

We both shook our heads "No!"

Dad frowned and said, "Get back on your bikes and go thank Wes. You always need to thank someone when they give you a gift."

We knew that, but we were both pretty shy away from the family.

So, off we went back to the Ford dealership and said, "Thank you for the shirts."

Wes smiled and said, "Where's Jackie?"

He was at church camp.

"I'm sure he'd like a shirt. Here, take this Country Squire shirt for him."

We now had another opportunity to thank Wes as we grabbed the shirt for Jackie and rode home.

Mark's birthday. Kathleen, Gary, Mom, Nancy, and Mark.

Once a week our phone rang with someone from the *Turtle Mountain Star* on the line asking for news. Mother would respond that we visited her parents farm last Sunday or that Dad's brother Harry had visited us from Portland, Oregon, etc. The next week this information showed up in print, and this was the page my mom turned to first when the *Star* arrived each week. This was the original Facebook.

The *Grand Forks Herald*, on the other hand, was a big deal. Originating in Grand Forks, 166 miles away, it was a daily paper that contained news of the nation and world, and was very important to local residents. Delivering the paper was one of the few paid jobs a kid could have in our town, so Jackie felt fortunate when he got a route. His customers were spread all over town.

Delivery on a hot summer day on his bike was manageable, but in the winter, with the frigid winds blowing and the temperatures below zero, pulling a toboggan piled with newspapers up the hills in town must have made Jackie question whether the rewards were worth it.

He picked up his papers each afternoon from the post office, a couple of buildings down from our store on Main Street. His customers paid 35 cents a week for seven days of news delivered to their porch and left inside their screen door. At the end of each month, he received a bill for his papers, so he needed to have collected money from his customers to pay his debt.

This task sounded easy, but Jackie learned to dread the collection process. Sometimes his knock on the door resulted in no response. Then there were those brave souls who answered the door and had no cash on hand to pay. I'm sure some customers had their money ready to pay him at month's end, but I remember mother often reminding him that she needed to write a check to pay for the papers and he needed to get the collecting done to reimburse her. When the bill was paid, Jackie got what was left: If a customer didn't pay, it hurt Jackie's wallet, not the newspaper's.

If Jackie finished his route and had leftover papers, he would take them across the street to the Vendome Hotel and walk through the lobby to sell his papers to the town's visitors. A couple of times during the winter, I accompanied him on his route. I still remember how long and cold the walk was.

I could help him by running up to a porch with a paper. Sometimes barking dogs made me afraid to go to a few porches. The physical effort of the daily trudge and the extreme temperatures convinced me that it was probably a good thing that girls were not allowed to have paper routes.

One winter afternoon, I returned to our apartment to find Mom putting a green-and-white checked wool cap on Jackie's head. It had a bill with a small green satin bow in the middle and ear flaps. The flaps were tucked into the cap now, but available to pull down to keep your ears warm on a cold day.

I hung up my coat and without thinking said, "Where'd you get the Canadian cap, Jackie?"

Mom turned and flashed me "the look," which, of course, wasn't a good thing. Jackie frowned and looked totally disgusted.

Mom said, "Gong, Jackie needs a new winter hat and we have these in the store and I don't appreciate your comments."

Jackie mumbled, "I hate this hat."

Mother looked at me in disgust as I said, "But it does look like a Canadian cap."

Then she smiled, because she knew I was right. It looked like a nice warm hat a middle-aged man would wear, and we always associated plaids with Canadians. This cap was not right for Jackie. It was dorky. Why would Jackie want to wear that?

Mother sighed and took Jackie's cap off. "Gong, you can be such a shit sometimes!" she said.

She took the cap and walked out the back door to the store. Jack was now indebted to me for life. I took the heat and he never had to wear that horrid cap. Mom told this story for years when she wanted her friends to see what she put up with at home.

That spring, I woke to the voice on the radio announcing that the day's temperature would be in the high thirties. This would be a warm one. The mellow voice of Nat King Cole, one of my Dad's favorite singers, crooned, *It Was Only a Paper Moon.*

"Time to eat!" called my mom from the kitchen.

I climbed down from my bed, narrowly missing Mark's curled body snoozing under a quilt on the bunk below. I almost tripped on Nancy's crib as I grabbed my clothes and walked through the bedroom door to the kitchen table.

Grabbing a clean turtleneck and underwear from the third drawer in the family chest of drawers, I started the automatic task of dressing: underpants, undershirt, garter belt, long brown cotton stockings, turtleneck, corduroy pants, and saddle shoes. My two older brothers were going through a similar ritual as we all prepared for another day of school.

Jackie was a seventh grader, Gary was in the fourth grade, and I was a second grader. Our apartment was warm thanks to the oil burner in the corner of the room, which chased the cold from the house. Mom's fragrant coffee filled the air as I sat down to my oatmeal. Mother was sitting at the head of the table feeding Nancy when Mark appeared at the door half asleep, but ready to attack a new day.

Breakfast was fast, as there was no time to dawdle. A brush was run through our hair, and we put on our parkas, grabbed our books, and were out the door. No snow pants or scarf over the face today, as it was a warm one.

The sun gleaming off the packed snow on the sidewalk was inspiring as our boots crunched on the snowy ground. We walked past the front of Dad's store and through the sleepy town slowly coming to terms with the day. The walk to school was nine or ten blocks, and we made the trek no matter what the weather. It was often cold and windy, and crystals of icy snow in our faces was not unusual.

Today was a bright day, and we walked quickly, stopping at times to stomp in a puddle or chase a wayward cat from our path. Jackie and Gary were always way ahead of me, often racing each other to school.

As we opened the massive school doors, we were greeted by the sounds of snow-booted students from first grade to high school seniors talking, shoving, and laughing as they walked to their classrooms. My day buzzed along, and soon it was time to put on parkas and boots and walk home. The day continued to be a bright one with just the slightest breeze.

The walk home was an adventure. I could choose my route from several possibilities and take time to climb on the dark-streaked snow piles created in the past weeks by the snowplow. The snow was days old by now. It was no longer the fresh white mounds, but crusted, mud streaked heaps that were beginning to melt. I made snow balls, blasted a few at trees, and sauntered home. The afternoon light was staying with us longer, and to imagine that winter may be in a decline was exciting.

Main Street had come alive. The excitement of living right in the heart of town never left me. Walking into the Ben Franklin Five and Dime Store, I examined the red, green, and yellow pencils, and found some new plastic flowered barrettes I thought I might need. I spun the comic book rack to see if there were new titles.

Down the street, I walked into the hotel lobby. The drapes were a rich, velvety material and the chairs, large and elegant. There were two men in business suits deep in discussion, while another man was reading the *Grand Forks Herald* in the large, wingback chair.

Okay, probably time to cross the street to see my dad. As I walked outside, out of the corner of my eye, a blurred image flashed by. I turned my head to see what it was and nearly screamed with delight! A red-breasted robin had landed on the roof of Hagen's grocery store. I was bursting with excitement as I ran up the three stairs to our store.

When I entered, I ran to my dad shouting, "I saw a robin. A robin flew onto Bernie's store. The harbinger of spring!"

My dad laughed as he counted out change for his customer, a member of our church buying a new house dress. She laughed, too.

"It's about time this winter is over," she said. "They are all too long. Maybe spring is coming."

The harsh winter was ending. I couldn't wait to go upstairs and tell my Mom. The birds were returning.

That summer, the sisters that lived in one of our building's front apartments moved out. We now had some room for expansion. Dad and Jackie moved the boys' bunk beds into the front apartment bedroom, and the bunk beds Mark and I slept in were placed on the floor side-by-side in the living room of the vacant apartment, just across from the oil burner. This apartment was really cold and would only be used for sleeping.

Dad took down the temporary wall he had used to provide a room for Jackie and Gary in our main apartment, and suddenly the living room grew. With our bunk beds out of Mom and Dad's room, Nancy's crib moved into their place and there was room to walk in the bedroom. This was progress.

Summer meant baseball. Jackie was a huge Brooklyn Dodgers fan, and so Gary and I were, too. Jackie rarely missed listening to a game on the radio, and he knew all the players and kept careful statistics of each game. How many times did a player bat, how many hits and how many runs took place each inning, and who made an error? Gary and I often listened to the games, too, as Jackie's enthusiasm was quite contagious.

"Why do you always want the Dodgers to win, Gong?" My friend Sharon Balwig asked one warm summer afternoon. "My dad likes the Yankees. He says they win the most games, so why don't you like the Yankees?"

This question stopped me in my tracks. Why did I like the Dodgers so much?

"I don't know why we like the Dodgers so much. The Yankees do win the most games, but at our house we always like the Dodgers best. I have to ask Jackie why."

I ran up the stairs to our apartment hoping to find him listening to a ball game. Sure enough, as I entered, he was lying in front of the radio with his notebook in front of him, charting the hits, runs, and errors for each player. Pee Wee Reese was up to bat and then it would be Duke Snider's turn. When there was a pause for a commercial, I asked him why we liked the Dodgers best.

"Come on, Gong. You know they have the best players and they have Jackie Robinson."

We all were aware of the challenges Jackie Robinson faced as the first black Major League Baseball player. He had some rough days with crowds taunting him as we listened to the radio, and he was the nicest guy. We were always for him and the Dodgers. Even though the Yankees almost always won, we were for the underdog. Jackie really liked Duke Snider, Gil Hodges, and Roy Campanella. In 1955, the Dodgers won their first World Series. It was unbelievable! We were all sitting in front of the radio cheering them on. Our loyalty had been rewarded. We knew the Dodgers were winners!

14.

Starting Down the Slippery Slope

Rolla, North Dakota
1955

"When you come to the end of your rope, tie a knot and hang on." —Unknown

Saturday was my favorite day, and this was a warm one. Jackie and Gary were playing baseball at Allen Brown's house, and my task after lunch each day was to put Mark down for his nap. Mark was almost three now, and Mother was taking care of Nancy, who was a toddler. After Mark fell asleep I was free, and since it was Saturday, Mom had given me a quarter to go to the movie.

The routine was to read Mark his three favorite books, lie down on the bed beside him, cuddle, rub his back, close my eyes pretending to be asleep, and listen for his breathing to slow and then for him to fall asleep. Next, remove my arm from around him, slowly and carefully move off the bed, quietly put on my shoes, gently open the door, and slowly walk out and close the door. Listen to make sure he didn't wake up, take a deep breath, smile, and know that it's great to be eight and the fun is about to begin!

Nancy's first birthday.

The theater was just a block away from our store on Main Street. I flew down the twenty-five stairs on the outside of our building, feeling the warmth of the sun and breathing in the gas fumes and exhaust from Fortune Martel's City Service gas station next door. He was busy today, but then, it was Saturday.

There was excitement in the air. I dodged folks carrying groceries from Hagen's store next door and a couple of ladies checking out dresses in Clara Rohr's window. I was on a mission. I crossed the street and could almost smell the theater's popcorn. I was there, number five in line to get my ticket. With ticket in hand, I took the 15 cents of change and ordered a small popcorn.

What was today's movie? I didn't know or care. The newsreel was still playing as my eyes adjusted to the darkened theater. Fantastic! I hadn't missed the cartoon. There was a man on the screen in a giant metal tube called an iron lung, and a voice-over spoke:

> Polio continues to be our greatest threat as thousands of children are crippled each year. The disease has no cure and no identified causes. Dr. Jonas Salk's vaccine trials are underway. 1.8 million children will participate in field tests in the United States and Finland.[1]

Next came the Mickey Mouse cartoon. Then the magic continued as Elizabeth Taylor appeared in a color movie titled *Elephant Walk*. Huge elephants were destroying a plantation in the jungle. Elizabeth Taylor in vividly colored gowns was kissing, screaming, smiling. I munched on.

A couple of weeks later my mom told me that my third grade class was selected to receive the first Salk polio vaccinations. Even though it was summer, I would need to go to my classroom and be vaccinated.

"Go down and tell Dad that he needs to be at the school with you on Tuesday at two o'clock. They want him to take a picture for the *Star*."

"You mean I have to get a shot?"

---

1. Christopher J. Rutty, PhD, "Herculean Efforts: Connaught and the Canadian Polio Vaccine Story," *CONNTACT* 9, no. 3 (1996); accessed at http://www.healthheritageresearch.com/Polio-Conntact9606.html

"Yes, your whole class does. This is very important. This vaccine can save kids from polio."

"Will it hurt?"

"It will hurt for a minute, but you've had shots before. Run and tell Dad!"

My stomach started to churn. I wasn't so sure about this. I wanted to stop polio, but why wasn't the fourth-grade class selected? When I got back upstairs, Jack and Gary were home and had heard the news.

"Of course, they would pick third-graders. They're all expendable!" Jackie crowed.

Gary chimed in, "I'm glad I don't need to get a shot. I hate shots!"

"What's expendable?" I asked Mom.

With a sigh, Mom said, "Jackie, go to Hagen's and get some milk for Nancy. She needs a bottle before her nap."

Jackie was reaching for the radio dial, "Aw, Mom! It's time for the Dodger game."

"You can be back in five minutes. Go, or I'll show you who's expendable!"

"It was just a joke!"

"Go!"

The threat of polio has been so diminished by the effectiveness of the vaccine that the only time you hear it mentioned anymore is when a new mother is going through the process of getting her baby inoculated. We hear varying degrees of concern about the effect of the vaccine on the child, but thankfully, we give no thought to the disease.

The world of the 1950s was very different, as polio was the century's most feared illness. It would strike without warning, and because it was so contagious, long periods of quarantine required separating families. Nearly 60,000 children were infected in 1952, thousands were paralyzed, and there were over 3,000 deaths. Vaccinations began in 1955, and by 1979, the polio virus had been eliminated in the United States.[2]

That Sunday, Dad brought up several pictures he had taken of my class getting our shots and there I was, back row and center with an apprehensive look on my face. The previous Tuesday afternoon, the smell of rubbing alcohol filled the classroom as we stood like little soldiers in a line, waiting for our chance to save the world from polio.

---

2. Jason Beaubien, "Wiping Out Polio: How the U.S. Snuffed Out a Killer," *Shots: Health News from NPR*, October 25, 2012.

Our first polio vaccinations.

During that school year, Mom and Dad were considering other employment options. They looked at other stores or restaurants to own. They were often preoccupied as they tried to determine the best path to take since the store was not working out financially. In two years of running the store, they found that they could make a living, but nothing more. We were very crowded in our apartment, and they still had no savings for a house. Following Grandpa Johnson's lead, education was a priority for them. How could they ever put five children through college?

Nancy continued to be a happy and easy child, but she often had ear infections. Dr. Goodman referred her to an

Eye, Ear, Nose, and Throat Specialist in Minot, about two hours away, so Mom and Dad took a couple of trips there to get a proper diagnosis and treatment for her.

One morning that summer, I went to the Balwigs' house after breakfast and fell asleep on Sharon's bed. Her mom woke me, felt my warm head, and said, "Gong, you have a fever. You need to go home and tell your mom that you're not feeling well."

Mom checked me when I got home and called the doctor. My temperature was 103 degrees, and that afternoon I was admitted to the hospital. Sister Bertha guided me to a bed, where I spent the next five days recuperating. I slept almost constantly for the first few days, the only interruption coming when it was time for a penicillin shot. This new drug had worked well during World War II[3] and by the time I was discharged, my bottom was black and blue from this miracle treatment that cured me.

Mom was very busy at home during this time, so I saw very little of her. One day as I started to improve, she arrived with a strawberry milkshake and a coloring book and colors for me. I missed everyone and couldn't wait to go home.

In September, the folks decided to take the 200-mile drive to Bismarck, to check out a Bob's Big Boy Drive-in Restaurant. This was a new dining concept and one of the

---

3. http://www.discoveriesinmedicine.com/Ni-Ra/Penicillin.html

first in North Dakota. The restaurant had opened a year earlier and did not have indoor seating, but was a drive-through service.

Car ownership was on the rise, and some families even had two cars. Bob's served double-decker hamburgers, fries, and malts. The folks were eager to see what this was all about. They planned to take Mark and Nancy to their babysitters, the Herrelas, while we were in school that day and then drive to Bismarck.

I started running a fever the night before. I was achy, and my throat and neck area were tender. The next morning my face was swollen with mumps. The fever continued, so Mom put a dish towel around my face, tying it at the top of my head so the swollen glands had support. Then she made a bed for me in the back seat of the car and off we went.

When we arrived at Bismarck, we drove to a window at Bob's and ordered three hamburgers, fries, and milkshakes. Mom and Dad went in and spent some time with the owner talking about the business, while I fell back asleep. I missed the conversation on the way home, but the idea of owning a drive-in restaurant did not come up again.

We all noticed a change in the atmosphere of the house. The folks often spent time in the evening trying to figure out what to do. The thought of moving was unsettling and scary, but each month's sales in our store confirmed what they already knew, that they had to do something else to support five children. The reality was that Rolla left no options for Dad as far as career opportunities.

Later that year on a cold and snowy Friday afternoon in early December, Jackie was preparing to go to his friend Janice Olson's house to have dinner with some classmates. He had become a teenager on his birthday that November, and we were all excited about him having dinner with friends. In our book, it was such a grown-up thing to do.

Janice lived a couple of blocks from us, just down the back stairs, out the back door through the parking lot and alley, turn right by the creamery and down a block. Her mom was making dinner for the kids and then they were going to play some games. Jackie bundled up in his snow pants, parka, and gloves.

As he was leaving for the party, Mom called, "Have fun, Jackie!"

You could actually see Jackie bristle as a frown appeared on his face and his shoulders tightened. "It's Jack, Mom! Don't call me Jackie!"

"Okay, Jack! Have fun!"

Mom relieved Dad in the store so he could come up for dinner, and then he and Mom switched places. When we finished eating, Mom brought the washtub in from the landing and was giving Mark and Nancy their baths in the kitchen when the door opened and Jack appeared earlier than expected. He was covered with snow and had a pained look on his face. His brow was furrowed, and he bit his lip as he took off his coat and boots. Mom was suddenly alert! She wrapped Nancy in a towel and handed her to me.

She rushed to him and asked, "What's the matter, Jack?"

He sat down on the couch and put his head in his hands. "I feel awful!" he said.

We all stared at Jack as Mother went over and put her arms around him.

"My God! You're hot!" she said, as he started to shake.

"What hurts?" she asked.

"I think this is the worst headache I've ever had. My neck hurts and now I'm freezing."

Jack is a teenager.

"Oh, Lumpy. Lay down and I'll get the thermometer and aspirin. You must have the flu."

She was back in a flash. We watched her every move. Jack's temperature was 103 degrees. Mom got his pajamas and grabbed the Vicks VapoRub. They both left our apartment and walked down the hall to the next apartment, where the four of us slept.

As soon as she left, Gary said, "He must be sick if he let Mom call him 'Lumpy!'"

Mom was always busy and she could be tough, but if you were sick, she was the sympathetic, concerned adult we all wanted and needed. Gary was right, though. Now that Jack was a teenager, he usually wouldn't put up with being called "Lumpy!" I started to worry. He must feel awful!

The next morning Jack was no better, so Mom called Dr. Goodman. His office wasn't open on Saturday, but being the only doctor in town meant he was always on duty, officially or not. He drove over and we watched anxiously as he examined Jack. The headache and fever had persisted and finally, with a shrug of his shoulders, Dr. Goodman said he didn't know what the problem was, but Jack would have to be admitted to the hospital for tests.

In a matter of minutes, Mom and Jack were in Dr. Goodman's black Cadillac driving to the hospital as more snowflakes began to fall. Just after noon Mom returned and said Jack was sleeping in the hospital and Sister Bertha was in charge. Dr. Goodman and Sister Bertha had given him a spinal tap and were waiting for results.

After dinner that night, Mom put on her heavy green storm coat. The temperature was below zero and the wind was blowing the frigid air off the prairie. She was meeting with Dr. Goodman and Sister Bertha at the hospital.

Before she left she gave me and Gary her usual instructions: "Take care of Mark and Nancy and behave!"

We turned on the radio and listened to the *Lone Ranger* and then continued with *Captain Midnight* as we entertained Mark and Nancy with Lincoln Logs. After an hour or so, Nancy started to rub her eyes and cry, so I got her bottle and rocked her to sleep. As I walked into Mom and Dad's bedroom to put her in her crib, I heard a noise outside. It was coming from the back stairs that led from the store below to the laundry landing. I heard it again. What was it? It wasn't loud, but someone was out there. While the radio announcer was describing the joys of drinking Chase & Sanborn Coffee, I tiptoed to the door and listened. It was a whimper. Was a cat or dog out there?

Slowly, I opened the door and there was my mom standing by the spin dryer crying. My heart was suddenly pounding! My mother did not cry often, and why didn't she come in the house? It was freezing out here! Her head was bent down toward the floor as she wiped her nose with a tissue.

I walked over to her and asked, "Mom! What's the matter?"

She hugged me to her damp coat still sprinkled with snow and sniffed and sobbed, "Jack has polio!"

15.

The Eye of the Hurricane

Rolla, North Dakota
1955

"Promise me you'll always remember: You're braver than you believe and stronger than you seem and smarter than you think." —A.A. Milne

The news of Jack's diagnosis spread quickly throughout Rolla.

"Mary, did you hear that Jack Holstad has polio?"

"Oh no! That's awful. Poor Lyda!"

"Well, I took my kids to the hospital yesterday afternoon to visit Jim's Dad and as we were leaving, we walked by Jack's room. Several of his friends were with him, and Sister Bertha was not happy. They were having a good time as Jack was lying there with his arm over his eyes. She whisked them out of the room and told them in no uncertain terms that Jack was very sick and that they needed to go home.

Now Hazel just called and said he has polio. I'm really worried about our kids. We were right outside Jack's room."

"Well, it is very contagious, Helen, but I always thought it was a summer illness. Where are they taking him?"

"Maurice and Lyda are driving him in Dr. Goodman's Cadillac to Fargo."

"Well, I'll be jiggered... and in this weather. That will be quite a trip! What are they doing with the other kids?"

"I haven't heard, but I'll check with Anne. She'll probably know."

"I just can't believe it. Jack is our paper boy, you know. Sometimes I've seen him coming up our hill in the worst storms pulling that toboggan filled with newspapers. At times, I check his progress against the telephone poles to see if he is actually moving. He always got the paper here and then the next day, he was back at it again. He's a good kid. I'm sorry he is so sick, but this could affect a lot of our kids!"

"Yes, I'll check with Anne and see what she knows. Why don't you check with Millie Mae."

"Okay."

"Goodbye."

Our phone started ringing early Sunday morning as news of Jack's diagnosis swept through the town. Friends called to see what was next for Jack's treatment, and offers of sympathy and help kept Mom and Dad busy as they tried to figure out the plan for the family.

That morning Dr. Goodman made a few calls to Fargo discussing Jack's symptoms and test results with doctors at St. John's Hospital, an 87-bed facility. This was huge compared to our hospital.

Since polio was the initial diagnosis, it was agreed that Jack would be admitted there for further testing and treatment. Dr. Goodman stopped by our apartment and talked to the folks. He offered them his black Cadillac for the two-hundred-forty-mile drive. His car was larger than our Ford, and Jack would be more comfortable in the back seat. The date was December 10, 1955, so road conditions and winter weather would be a challenge.

Mrs. Herrala agreed to take Mark and Nancy now. Mom could concentrate on Jack knowing that Mrs. Herrala was in charge of her two babies.

Anne Dunlop offered to take me and Gary. We were thrilled to stay with the Dunlops. Mrs. Youtz, whose husband ran the bank, also had a baby, so she called and offered Mother a load of clean diapers so the folks could get on their way without having to do laundry. Cloth diapers were all we had in 1955, and since we didn't have a dryer, this saved Mom hours.

Gary and I packed a bag, and with tears running down her face Mom gave us a hug as we were dropped off at the Dunlops. This had been a whirlwind day and now seeing Mother so upset and Dad with a worried look on his face,

I wanted to cry, too. Our family was falling apart. Mom and Dad took off in the big black Cadillac with snowflakes falling on the windshield. Jack was lying in the back seat with his eyes closed.

On the way to the hospital, Mom and Dad stopped at Mom's sister Ellen's home in Grand Forks, about two-thirds of the distance to Fargo. Jack remembers Mom and Dad going into Ellen and Warren's house, and our cousins Bill and Jim and some of their buddies running out of the house to see the impressive black Cadillac and to visit with Jack. There seemed to be no concern about Jack being contagious.

When they reached Fargo and St. John's Hospital, Jack was immediately placed in isolation. No one could enter his room without putting on a gown and washing all exposed areas with a sterile solution. The same procedure was followed when leaving the room. My parents spent a couple of days at the hospital with Jack, and after more testing, the diagnosis was changed from polio to mumps and encephalitis.

Encephalitis is a viral inflammation of the brain tissue. While there was relief that Jack didn't have polio, this was also a serious disease. With a heavy heart, my parents had to leave Jack and return to Rolla.

Meanwhile, in the little apartment above the store, we were all worried about Jack. His empty chair at the table every night brought us all down. He was so far away in a room all by himself; it was solitary confinement. Christmas preparations were minimal as we waited to hear when he would be coming home.

Jack was well taken care of in the hospital, but it was very difficult for him being away from family and friends. He created great friendships with the nursing staff, who took the lonely child under their wing. Two of his favorites were Gloria Jeston and Tillie Mack. The nurses brought him peanuts they purchased from the vending machine for a nickel.

Jack's room was stark and sterile, and the only source of entertainment was a coin-operated radio. I remember Mother sending dimes to Jack so he could listen to the radio for an hour. He had an earpiece that he could place under his pillow and listen to his favorite disk jockey, the Jack of Diamonds, who played songs he enjoyed. We sent him letters, and he received packets of letters from his classmates in Rolla, but his days were long and lonely.

When Jack could sit up in bed, he spent time tallying the cars that went by his hospital window. There were more cars in Fargo in a day than we saw in Rolla in a year, so he counted the number of Fords, Chevrolets, and Pontiacs that passed by. Television wasn't available yet in hospitals, but Jack had a window and he could chart cars.

Jack had seven spinal taps while at St. John's. This procedure is also called a lumbar puncture because a needle is inserted into the spinal canal in the lower back to collect fluid.[1] The fluid is then examined and a pus count is taken to determine the degree of inflammation in the brain.

Several days before Christmas, Jack's doctor came to him and said, "I hope you have a stiff upper lip because your spinal taps are not clear and you will not be going home for Christmas."

Jack had been counting the days until Christmas. We all felt certain he would be home by then. Now tears rolled down his face as he prepared for a Christmas alone in his room.

Mother took the phone call from St. John's telling her Jack would not be home and she started crying. She got off the phone, sat at the table, put her head down, and sobbed. We watched in silence.

In a few minutes, Mother sat up and stammered, "It is such a worry to have a sick child. It is just killing me that I can't visit him. He's all alone in that hospital miles and miles away with roads that we can't even get through. We can't leave the store, we can't leave you kids and he's not getting well as quickly as I had hoped. What is happening to us? I don't know if we're coming or going anymore with the store.

---

[1]. https://www.mayoclinic.org/tests-procedures/lumbar-puncture/about/pac-20394631

Should we move? How can we even think about Christmas? What else can go wrong?"

With that, Nancy woke up from her nap, and I went in to change her diaper and get her up. Mother had no energy to take care of our baby. That evening her flashing lights started and very soon she was in bed with a migraine headache. She would not be feeling well for a couple of days.

Outside our window Rolla was blanketed in snow. Christmas wreaths decorated Main Street, and our little town looked like a scene from a Norman Rockwell Christmas card. The outdoor peace and tranquility was in complete contrast to life in our apartment.

Winter storms continued and snow was piled everywhere. Mom was feeling more in control and told me they had ordered a doll for my Christmas present, but that it and other gifts would be delayed because the packages from Sears couldn't be delivered.

Jack was improving and just needed a clear spinal tap, which would probably happen soon. We needed to delay Christmas until Jack got home and we could all be together. We all loved Christmas, but seeing the strain on Mom and Dad over the last few months, we just wanted some stability, which would certainly come when Jack returned home.

Once again Jack's nurses came to his rescue. Nurse Tillie gave him a book, *Lucky to Be a Yankee*, by Joe DiMaggio.

She knew how much Jack loved the Dodgers and hated the Yankees, so there was a little jab there, but he read and appreciated the book. Of course, it didn't change his opinion of the Dodgers, but he recognized that his nurses were trying to make the best of a tough situation.

I don't know why Mom and Dad continued trying to figure out their future plans while our family life at home was so unsettled. Perhaps the store's lease needed to be renewed early the next year. Anyway, Dad decided to take advantage of our delayed celebration, and the next morning he told us that he and Gary were going to take the train to Portland, Oregon. He was going to try to find a job in Portland. If so, we would probably be moving to Oregon the next year.

At that time Portland had a population of almost 400,000. Certainly, in a city that large Dad could find work. Dad's brother Harry lived there with his wife Elsie, so we already knew someone. The thought of a move came as a total shock to me. How could we leave Rolla, our store, our school, our friends, our grandparents, and our cousins? Each day seemed to bring worse news, but most of all we needed Jack to come home.

Eating in the dining car on the train was far too expensive, so Mom roasted a turkey and made enough turkey sandwiches to get Dad and Gary to Portland. In a few days, they left to ride the Great Northern Dome Liner.

They could sit in the viewing cars and see all the sights on their way to Portland.

Their trip sounded exciting to me, and I wanted to go, too, but I stayed home to help Mother with Mark and Nancy. Mom had to run the store without Dad and take care of us and worry about Jack.

Just before dinner on Sunday evening, our phone rang and I ran to answer it. It was Anne Dunlop. Mom was starting to get dinner ready, and when I told her Anne was on the line, her eyes lit up.

"Hi Anne!" she said. "No, Jack will not be able to come home. His last spinal tap wasn't clear and so he can't be discharged. I felt so bad for him. Not only does he not feel well with those awful headaches, but he is so alone there. I've never felt so helpless! I am so worried about him, but there is no way I can go there. I have the store to run and when Maurice left for Portland, the reality of our move really hit me. We will delay Christmas which is the least of my worries, but I feel like we're churning. The stability we've always known is now gone. We have to get Jack home and the thought of closing the store and moving to another part of the country is overwhelming. Where do we begin?"

Mom and Anne talked for awhile before Mom continued making dinner.

Later that night, as we were finishing washing the dishes, Mom told me to get Nancy ready for bed.

With a frown I said, "Why do I have to do everything? Gary gets to go on a trip, Jack gets to be in Fargo, and I have to be here."

Even as I said the words, I knew this would not end well. The next thing I knew, Mom slapped my face very firmly and told me to straighten up and get Nancy's pajamas. She had tears running down her face.

"These are trying times, Gong. Don't ever think that Jack is having fun. He's all alone in an isolation ward miles away. I cannot deal with a bratty child here at home. You need to help me."

With my face stinging and tears running down my cheeks, I picked up Nancy as she softly patted the red handprint on my face. This is a clear memory for me because I don't recall my mother ever slapping me before this or after.

In a few minutes, Mom returned to the bedroom and sat on the bed with her head in her hands.

In a tired voice she said, "I'm getting flashing lights, Gong!" She was exhausted, and I felt doubly guilty now for saying something so stupid and adding to her distress. Mother was getting another migraine headache.

She had given Mark his bath, so I helped get him into his warm pajamas. Mother got Nancy's bottle, put her in her crib, and then prepared to go to bed herself. Vicks

VapoRub on the forehead, a damp cloth on her head, an aspirin, and a dark room were what Mom needed now.

Since the boys were both gone, Mom let me and Mark sleep in the living room, rather than going down the hall by ourselves to our sleeping apartment. Mark and I would sleep on the couch. With a heavy heart, I closed Mom's bedroom door. Mark was holding his favorite book, *The Happy Man and His Dump Truck*, ready for the bedtime reading ritual.

The house was silent except for the hum of the oil burner fan and the wind blowing snow against the window. Our little Christmas tree stood in a corner, with its red and green lights shining. Gary and I had decorated the tree a couple of weeks earlier, and the branches looked like they were dripping with silver icicles. We liked the effect, but now I realized we had probably overdone it. Needles were dropping to the floor, and I hoped the tree could hang on for a while longer.

We all needed to maintain for a few more days. The calendar told us that Christmas was December 25, and I had been counting the days. Now I knew Christmas would come when the family was finally back together. It had been a strange year with Jack's illness, and now Gary and Dad were checking out a new city for us to live in.

Christmas wasn't about my new doll. I just wanted us to have a normal life again. I felt like I was in a tiny boat lost at sea in the eye of a hurricane. I was only eight and was thinking about the good old days when I did the banking for my dad, and ran up and down the street pretending to be Sister Bertha. Now everything was changing.

Mark and I got under the heavy quilts, and I read him the book. I turned out the lights, and as I cuddled him, I reminded myself that I needed to help Mother tomorrow. I also needed to quit saying stupid things. Maybe tomorrow would be better.

16.
Off and Running

Rolla, North Dakota
1956

"Is it just me or does anyone else think we're stuck in a snow globe and some jerk keeps giving it a shake?"
—Anonymous

"Momma, Daddy, and Jack are home!" shouted Mark, who was stationed at the living room window waiting for the first glimpse of our car as the folks returned with Jack from their two-hour drive from the Devils Lake train station.

Nancy, now almost two years old, with Mom's naturally curly blonde hair and Dad's brown eyes, was toddling around the living room, helping me and Gary pick up Tinkertoys. We wanted to make sure the house was ready for the celebration. This was Jack's homecoming party and our Christmas, so you know it was a red-letter day for all of us. Jack had been gone for almost a month, and now his seat at the table would be filled.

The road conditions that winter were still unpredictable, so when Jack's spinal tap was finally clear, he was discharged from St. John's Hospital. A cab was called, and with unsteady legs, Jack began the trip to the train station with the falling snow adding to the freezing temperature. He bought a ticket for Devils Lake, sat on the wooden bench, and waited for his train to arrive.

Jack was thirteen, but not ready for so many adult responsibilities. He would have loved to have the folks pick him up at the hospital and acknowledge the pain, the fear, and the silence of the last month, but that was not to be.

The loneliness continued for another few hours as he boarded the train. Jack had been in bed for a month. Now, between the excitement of finally being discharged and the limited walking he had done, he was exhausted. He dozed on the two-and-a half-hour ride.

When the conductor called out "Devils Lake" and the train screeched to a halt, Mom and Dad were there. Mom had tears in her eyes as she welcomed him home with a big hug. Jack was very thin, but his dimpled face was all smiles. His month of isolation was over. Dad grabbed Jack's bag, and the happy trio caught up on hospital life as they made their way home.

Dad and Gary had enjoyed the train ride to Portland and back. It was an easy trip and at times quite beautiful. The solitude of the ride gave Dad some quiet time to ponder options. He and Gary slept in their seats at night and avoided the expensive dining car, eating Mom's turkey sandwiches for each meal. They were impatient to get to Portland, stretch their legs, and have something different to eat.

Uncle Harry and Aunt Elsie met them at the Portland train station. They were eager to show them Portland, as they were hoping Dad would decide to move there. Dad checked out work possibilities and felt good about what he saw. He had talked to a photo studio that would probably have a job for him in March.

Elsie and Harry were motivated to help us find a house. There were several colleges around Portland, and the weather included lots of rain and little snow. A large city would offer Dad many opportunities.

With all that in mind, Mom and Dad decided to make the move. They planned to be living in Portland by March, so there was lots to do to get ready. Dad contacted Gamble-Skogmo's headquarters to give them notice that he was closing our store. They sent representatives out to help with the sale of all the merchandise.

Mother began figuring out what we would take with us and what we would leave behind. Dad brought our

Norwegian trunk up from the back of the store to start packing.

Gary remembers details of the truck Dad bought: a 1947 flatbed Ford with wooden sides and a V8 engine. It was green with a yellow grill. Dad bought a heavy-duty tarp that would cover everything on the truck and protect it from the weather.

I'm not sure why the folks decided to move during the winter months. Possibly, it was a job offer in Portland in March or maybe the lease on the store was about to expire, but the move would have been much easier if we hadn't been dealing with winter weather and starting a new school midyear.

A four-page supplement in the *Turtle Mountain Star* was printed announcing the sale of store merchandise:

> Closing Out Sale Opens February 2 at 9 A. M.
> Selling Out-Nothing Held. $20,000 stock sacrifice.
> Big Savings on Quality Merchandise.
> Store closed Tuesday and Wednesday to prepare for the sale. Come early for best buys.
> Skogmos-Rolla.

There was also a personal note on the inside the ad:

> Well, here she goes. The whole store. We're slashing prices and going out of business in Rolla. We're moving to Oregon where we will establish

a new store. We want to do this sale fast in order to move out to a new location we have in Oregon.

Sure we'll lose some money on this quick sale, but we want to get going. Yes, we'll have to sell the store out to the bare walls. Yes, we'll be sorry to leave Rolla, but we have a better location in Oregon, so the best to you good folks in Rolla.

Some of the sale items were: Women's dresses regular $8.95 were on sale for $4.77. Robes and house coats were $2.66. Men's hooded parkas regularly priced at $21.95 were on sale for $15.77. Ladies shoes including saddle oxfords regularly priced at $5.95 were on sale for $3.87. Cannon bath towels regularly priced at 69 cents were 38 cents.

Once the sale started, the store filled with customers searching for bargains, which kept Mom and Dad busy ringing sales. The store looked like a whirlwind had gone through it. For items that didn't sell, Dad called in an auctioneer and moved out more inventory. Finally, he sold the store fixtures and the very last of the merchandise to Mr. Hasen, who owned the Golden Rule Clothing Store down the street. By the end of the month, our store was empty.

It was eerie to see the bare bones of our store. I stood on the mezzanine, where Dad's large wooden roll-top desk used to be, looking down at our vacant building. The sweet baby clothes were gone, men's work pants were nowhere to be seen, women's hats so popular in the spring had vanished. All of the 8 x 10 inch framed children's photos that had encircled the store were gone.

Just days before it was filled with activity and energy, and now it was desolate. The walls, now freed of the varnished wood fixtures, showed their age and their need for repair. I loved this store. I had spent lots of days here helping Dad. Change was coming very quickly. I wasn't sure what moving meant, but right now everything felt lonely and chaotic.

"Class, please sit down! Boys and girls, take your seats! It's time for Kathleen's party!" said Mrs. Carlson.

My third-grade teacher's words sent my classmates to their desks, where they waited in eager anticipation for this unusual event: a going-away party for a classmate. The stable community of Rolla was well aware that Maurice and Lyda Holstad were selling their clothing store, packing up their five children, and moving to Portland.

I heard a customer discussing us the night before at Hagen's grocery store: "Whoever heard of going over the pass in March! This is not the time to drive over the mountains. What is Maurice thinking? Taking all those kids to Oregon?"

Macky Hagen responded, "He wants the kids to have a college education and doesn't think he can get it for them by staying here. All I know is, I will miss them all."

As I got the bottle of milk out of the chest refrigerator, I smiled. Macky would defend Dad. We were all going to miss her.

Back in our classroom, Mrs. Carlson called me to the front of the room and presented me with a blue plastic wallet and a red autograph book. She noted the blank look on my face as I opened the autograph book. She explained that everyone in the class should write something in it for me. She passed the book around the class, and in typical third-grade fashion, everyone signed their name. We were all naïve about the clever little sayings we would know by sixth grade.

After class was dismissed, we put on our parkas and boots. With gifts in hand, I left my school, walking out with Beverly Jackson. We talked on the way to her house as though this was just another day. Neither of us knew what moving really meant. When we came to her new, pink house, we waved goodbye and I walked on to Main Street and to our store. What would tomorrow bring? I wasn't sure.

Our neighborhood was always an extension of our family. Almost 65 years after we left Rolla, my dear friend Janice Dunlop wrote this note responding to a Christmas card I sent her family in 2014:

> Talk about a voice from the 'way, way back' past. Brought back so many girlhood memories with you and your family... I had few playmates in town except you and your brothers just one block away. Remember the Leonard kids close, too. I chuckled at you playing hide 'n go seek with your grandkids because we were probably still playing that when you left Rolla. I did a lot of grieving when your family moved away. How wonderful your parents were and good to me.

The last week in February was a moving frenzy. Dad's former deputy sheriff, Ernie Fortin, offered to drive our car to Oregon. Mother drove in Rolla but was very intimidated by the idea of driving in larger cities, especially with the winter road conditions. Dad would drive the truck. Herman Albright, another Rolla friend, offered to travel with us in his 1954 green Chevy pickup. We could load his pickup with our belongings and he would drive to Oregon with us. Then he would purchase plywood in Portland and drive back to Rolla and sell it. Ernie would ride home with him. It seemed to all be coming together.

Jack did not return to school that year. He was still in a weakened condition, and needed to rest and recuperate. He spent his days on the couch in the living room, listening to the radio, organizing his baseball card collection, drawing Disney-like cartoons for us, and reading.

Toward the end of February, on one of our last visits to Grandma and Grandpa Johnson's farm when all of Mom's family was in attendance, Aunt Pearl invited Jack to stay on her farm during the upcoming hectic and crazy moving days.

As we were about to leave, Grandpa took mother aside. "We want to give you your inheritance Lyde," he said. "It isn't much, but it will help you get started in Oregon."

Tears rolled down my mother's face. The memory of paying her Dad's taxes years ago flooded back to her. Now it was her turn to be on the receiving end. The future was so vague. How could she move so far from her beloved family?

"Oh Dad! Thanks. How can I get along without you?"

Grandpa gave her a firm hug as a tear rolled down his cheek and said, "You'll do fine, but we'll sure miss you."

There was not a dry eye among the adults in Grandpa's house as the Norwegian hugs and kisses were given. We were all sad to be leaving the cousins, aunts, and uncles that we loved. They were such an important part of our lives, and we had no idea when we would see them again.

In a few days, our truck and Herman's pickup were packed. We took some appliances, but very little furniture made the cut. Great Grandma's trunk, filled with clothes, was placed in a secure spot on the truck. Anxiety and sadness, reminiscent of the feelings our ancestors must have experienced, were written all over my mother's face. Put your future in your ability to work hard, have faith in the Lord, and then hang on to your hat!

After a very long day of packing, we slept in Rolla for the last time. The next morning we set off on our adventure to Oregon with mixed feelings. I had a sense of excitement as Dad led the way in the big truck, and Herman and Gary followed in the pickup. Ernie was behind the wheel of our Ford, with Mom beside him. Nancy, Mark, and I shared the back seat with Nancy's wooden potty chair. We drove down the road like a short parade as we set off on our journey.

We stopped at Aunt Pearl's farm on the way and picked up Jack, who joined Dad in the truck. Mom and Pearl hugged and cried.

Unfortunately, in all the confusion of leaving, Jack's precious baseball card collection did not make the move, a fact he lamented for years. We had one last stop at Grandma and Grandpa's farm for more hugs and tears, and then we were off and running.

On one hand, I was excited about a new adventure, but as I thought about it, I also felt fear and uncertainty. Where would the road take us? How could we live without our friends and family? I hugged Mark and Nancy close to me as we zoomed down the road.

17.
A Whole New World

North Dakota, Montana, Idaho, Oregon
1956

"You can never cross the ocean unless you have the courage to lose sight of the shore." —Anonymous

Our little caravan followed the grid through North Dakota and then into Montana. Before we got too far down the road, however, we all stopped at the Gambles store in Rugby. Dad parked the truck in front of the store as Herman and Ernie found places to park down the street. A few minutes later, Dad came out of the store with Nancy's first tricycle. Her second birthday had been overlooked in the confusion the week before. Dad found a place for the new tricycle in the truck, tightened the tarp, and checked the tires, and off we went. The shifter on the truck would periodically slip out of gear, so Jack or Gary, whomever was sitting with Dad on that day, was tasked with holding it in place.

We drove through flat and white snow-covered plains and foothills, with views of snow-capped mountains in the far distance. We passed small towns with water towers standing straight and tall, proudly announcing the town's name. Small farms whizzed by with their stately windmills and neat fences. Other farms had snow-covered, broken-down cars filling their yards. Black locomotives pulling miles of railroad cars across the lonesome plains looked like snakes slithering on their stomachs, searching for food.

Each day as it started to get dark, Dad, leading the procession in the truck, began looking for a motel with a kitchenette. Ideally there would be a couple of regular motel rooms and one with a kitchen so Mom could cook dinner for all of us.

Once the procession of vehicles was parked, Dad would take the car to the closest store and return with groceries for our dinner. His list usually consisted of hamburger, milk, bread, sandwich meat, and coffee.

That first night, Dad got Nancy's trike down from the truck before he left, so we all spent time helping her learn to ride her new toy. We ate, and then Herman and Ernie went to their room as we prepared for our night's rest. The next morning Mom or Dad fixed us a breakfast of eggs or pancakes, and we helped make sandwiches for everyone for lunch. Black coffee was made by the potful and a thermos was filled for each vehicle.

When we were slightly over four hundred miles from Rolla in Malta, Montana, the universal joint on the truck went out. Luckily, we weren't on top of the Rocky Mountains, but the parts for our truck were not available anywhere in town. We ended up spending a couple of days in the motel waiting for parts and then a few more days waiting for repairs to be completed. The added delay and the expense concerned the folks. We all wanted to get back on the road again, but as the trip continued, the heater in the truck quit working, so during those winter days, Dad and Jack or Gary nearly froze.

The scenery improved each day. Mom was very nervous about crossing the Rocky Mountains, but it went well and before we knew it, we were in Oregon. We had never seen so many trees. The ground and ridges were carpeted with massive, spectacular forests. The trees grew so close, it looked like one was almost on top of another. We met log trucks on the road transporting massive logs to lumber mills.

As we drove beside the swiftly moving Columbia River, we were amazed by the diversity of the scenery and the beauty of Oregon. We stopped briefly to see Multnomah Falls outside of Portland. It was magnificent! I had never seen a waterfall before. The water flowed over the ridge, settled in a pool, and then created a second waterfall. A bridge connected the falls, and the scene was completed by what must have been a million trees. Maybe this move wasn't so scary after all. I was seeing sights I had only seen pictures of before this trip.

It was late in the afternoon and we were beginning to lose daylight as we continued on into Portland. As we approached the city, I remember looking out the car window at the sea of lights. It was an epic scene. Was the glow in the sky welcoming us? There was no time to ponder this as Mother reacted to the stress of entering this metropolitan area.

"I'm trying to read this map and find our way to Elsie and Harry's," she said in a tense voice. "I want you all to sit still and be quiet!"

That familiar tone meant business, so Mark, Nancy, and I cuddled in the back seat as Ernie drove our car through the dusky, rainy evening. None of our drivers were used to traveling in a complex city like Portland, so they all felt the strain.

We drove down streets filled with traffic: cars, trucks, and buses. There were frequent traffic lights. Brakes screeched, horns honked, and whistles blew.

After a few wrong turns and several delays as all three of our vehicles couldn't make it through the green lights of several intersections at once, we arrived at Harry and Elsie's shipshape two-bedroom house. I breathed a sigh of relief. Mom set the map down, put her head in her hands, and began to relax. Ernie calmly smiled as he parked the car. Mark opened the door, ready to stretch his legs, with Nancy right behind him.

Harry and Elsie's house was a vision to behold. It sat on a compact corner lot, the boundaries defined by a chain-link fence with a modest gate at the center. Multicolored flowers snuggled next to the building, and everything was neat and tidy. We all ran in to meet our hosts. Ready or not, we were here!

Elsie had a hot dinner on the table for us. We hadn't seen her and Harry since they visited us for Grandpa Holstad's funeral, which now seemed an eternity ago. We were thrilled to see them, to enjoy their warm, organized house, and to think that step one of our trek was over. Completing our long journey was quite an accomplishment. Tomorrow was another day, but for now we could relax, be happy, and enjoy Dad's brother and his wife. Our family spent the night there, while Ernie and Herman stayed at a nearby motel.

The next morning, after breakfast, Harry and Elsie led us in their polished, black 1950 Ford a few miles down the road to a house they had rented for us on SE Foster Rd, in a rural part of town. There were no sidewalks and there was space between the homes. On one side of the road was an IGA store. Across the street and down a fairly steep driveway was our new home.

We quickly got out of the vehicles to examine it. Entering from the driveway, we found a kitchen with space for our washing machine, then a living room, three small bedrooms, and a bathroom with a tub, toilet and sink. No more going down the hall above the store to the toilet. This was very convenient.

The floors were covered with gray, six-inch square tiles. Harry turned on the heat to show us that the floors would get warm first, since the house was heated with hot water pipes under the concrete floor. We had never heard of such innovation. We had come a long way from our oil burner.

The living room had a fireplace across one end and a large window looking out at the driveway. The house was more than we had hoped for, and having a bathtub made us all want to test the waters.

Dad backed the truck right next to the door and then he, Harry, Herman, and Ernie began unloading the truck, filling the living room with boxes. Once they found some of the kitchen boxes, Elsie and Mom began organizing the kitchen. We unpacked some of our favorite toys, and the next couple of days flew by as we got settled into our new home.

Some packed boxes of items we didn't need right away were still sitting around the edge of the living room beside the Norwegian trunk, which was filled with our summer clothes. When the truck was empty, we said a tearful goodbye to Ernie and Herman as they left with the pickup filled with plywood. I didn't know Herman well, but hugging Ernie goodbye brought tears to my eyes. He was one of my best friends in the world. I watched the plywood-filled pickup drive down the road on its way back to Rolla, wondering when I would ever see my friend again.

The next day was Sunday. Mom and Dad went to a furniture store and came home with a few chairs, a double bed for their room, and a television set. Stores were never open in Rolla on Sunday, so this was unreal. In Portland, many stores were open later than 6 PM during the week, too, including the grocery store across the street. We were experiencing a new world.

When the folks returned, they placed a large square box in the center of the living room. We all gathered around as Dad opened it. Inside was a black metal twenty-four-inch Admiral television set that stood on four legs. I didn't know what television was. None of my friends in Rolla had one. Once, when we were at Aunt Pearl's house, they showed us a black-and-white television set that looked like a small box with a screen on it. The picture was blurred like it was taken in a snowstorm. They had gotten it in California, but since reception in North Dakota was so poor, I didn't understand what the big deal was.

Dad began to plug this monster in and adjust some dials, and there on the black-and-white screen was a Wheaties box. A voice told us we needed to eat the "Breakfast of Champions." I couldn't believe it. This was like having a small movie theater in our house. We still had no living room furniture, but we all gathered around this magical box, mesmerized. We sat on the floor, or found a wayward chair or a packing box to sit on as we marveled at this new technology. Details of moving in could certainly wait.

Mom had our closet filled, and she told us to take our baths early because the next day we were going to our new school. It was a treat to spend time in the bathtub and get our pajamas on while she prepared dinner.

Mom had bought a *TV Guide* at the IGA store and it told us that on Sunday night the *Ed Sullivan Show* was on. We could all watch it if we were ready for bed afterward. We quickly figured out whose turn it was to wash dishes. Jack, Gary, and I traded off: one washed, one dried, and one got a break. With dishes done, Mom found the pressure cooker kettle among the boxes and made popcorn as we all settled in to enjoy our first night of television.

Outside, the gloomy night was saturated with pounding rain, but inside, we had a fire in the fireplace and bowls of popcorn as Ed Sullivan came onto the stage. He introduced singers, dancers, a man telling jokes, and a man in a funny hat, balancing spinning plates on a couple of thin sticks. We were spellbound.

Next, a man named Ronald Reagan welcomed us to the GE Theater. He showed us lots of appliances, and then we watched a little play. Since tomorrow was our first school day, the fun ended here. Time to brush our teeth and get in our bunk beds.

As we lay in bed, the two bunk beds side by side in the room, I asked the boys, "Do you remember how to get to school?"

Mom and Dad had driven us to our new school several blocks away. I had looked out the car windows, but never thought about trying to find the school on Monday. They went in and registered us, but there were so many changes in the last few days, I couldn't remember how to get to school. It was a large school with several classes for each grade from first to eighth.

Jack said, "We can find it tomorrow, Gong. There will be a lot of kids at this school."

"I won't know any of them," I said as my stomach started to churn.

"None of us will," said Jack. "I wish we had our Rolla friends here."

"Well, the house is nice," I said, "Maybe the new kids will be nice, too."

"Portland is really weird," said Gary. "I miss Rolla, but, don't forget, after school we can watch TV."

On that happy thought, we drifted off to sleep, unaware of challenges that tomorrow would bring.

18.
Culture Shock

Portland, Oregon
1956

"You can't start the next chapter in your life if you're still rereading the last one." —Anonymous

Gilbert Elementary School was not a large, brick rectangle like the Rolla School. It was angular, and had a playground with large expanses of pavement and several carport-like coverings over patio areas.

We were dressed in our best clothes: pink and gray corduroy shirts and pants for the boys and my favorite red-checked school dress with my garter-belt clipped cotton stockings. We left the school office with a helper, who walked us to our classrooms. We took a winding path past three classrooms, through the gymnasium and up two flights of stairs before finally arriving.

"Here is your classroom, Kathleen," said the helper. "Third Grade, Mrs. Flanagan."

A tall, slender, pretty young woman opened the door and welcomed me. I was so confused. How did I get here? How could I find my way to this classroom tomorrow? Come to think of it, how do I find our house after school? What if I couldn't find the boys after school since I didn't know how to find our house?

These thoughts were going through my head as I entered my new classroom, filled with students seated at their desks in five straight rows, all staring at me. The room had a very high, slanted ceiling, and on one side, a row of clerestory windows had been placed two-thirds of the way up the wall.

Mrs. Flanagan introduced me to the class as my heart almost pounded through my chest. My hands were sweaty, and I was relieved when she took me back to a table at the edge of the room. She told me when she finished her morning activities, she would find a desk for me. I just sat at the table and glanced up at a bulletin board, hoping that very soon the sixty-two eyes staring at me would find another place to rest. If this was what moving meant, I just wanted this day to be over. I just wanted to go home to Rolla.

Mrs. Flanagan was talking to the class now, so I could look at the group and try to figure this place out. No one wore long stockings or corduroy shirts.

Mrs. Flanagan passed out a worksheet, and with pencils in hand, thirty-one heads focused on their task. She brought me some books and a pencil. She said nice things to me, but I just stared in silence. Then she gave me the worksheet, and I put pencil to paper.

A short time later she said, "Class, it's time for science. Please line up. Carol, you will be girls' line leader. Bob, you will lead the boys."

I walked to the girls' line and we left the room, once again walking as if in a maze until we reached the science room. A middle-aged woman in a green cardigan greeted us at the door and introduced herself as Mrs. Rogers. She took me to her desk and put my name in her attendance book. She noted my long, brown cotton stockings and asked me where I was from. There was no way I was going to tell her about my garter belt!

After I answered her questions, she took me to my desk. She began telling the class about the structure of rocks. She had ten rocks laid out on a row on a table and showed us the different strata, texture, and color. Science in Rolla meant getting out the 4" x 6" red cloth-covered book with SCIENCE on the cover. We would turn to page 29 and read about weather.

This science room was filled with equipment. There were scales, dark-colored bottles, strange-shaped glass jars, and microscopes. Before I knew it, we were done and it was time to line up and return to Mrs. Flanagan's room. That meant retracing our steps through the maze and confusion. How would I remember all this and find our new house?

Lunch was a blur in a room with many tables, trays you pick up and pass to the cooks, who fill your plate and give you a carton of milk. Sit down at a table. Eat and then rush off to the playground in a herd.

Once outside, girls in my classroom raced to the box of ropes. Rope jumping was the thing to do. Two girls grabbed the ends of a long rope and started turning, while other girls lined up to take their turn jumping. The group chanted rhymes in a sing-song fashion. I was intrigued. I had never jumped rope before. Our playground in Rolla was covered with snow most of the year. I heard:

> I like coffee
> I like tea
> I like the boys
> And the boys like me
> Yes, no, maybe so
> Yes, no , maybe so

The girls awaiting their turn chanted this, and the jumper continued until she missed. The best jumpers liked "Red Hot Peppers":

> Red Hot Pepper
> In the pot
> Gotta get over

What the leader's got: 10, 20, 30, 40…

The girls turning would speed up the rope until the jumper missed. The girl jumping kept track of her highest count. The person jumping would eventually trip, or slip, or stop and the next girl started a new rhyme.

I stood by a pole on a partially covered patio watching my new world. A couple more groups came running out of the cafeteria, and I scanned the playground looking for Gary. I didn't see him before the bell rang.

We lined up and walked through a different maze back to Mrs. Flanagan's room. The day wore on as I worried about how I would find Jack and Gary, and how we would find our house. The worksheets were fun, and the books were nice and plentiful, but not a moment too soon, it was time to line up one last time and go home.

I walked out into the rain and saw a blur of yellow raincoats on the playground. It looked like a brood of ducklings searching for their mothers. I tried to get my bearings. I could see two gates, and kids were everywhere.

"Think!" I told myself! "Focus! Which gate did we come in?"

I remembered walking by a jungle gym a hundred hours ago when we arrived. Okay, search the playground. To the right was the jungle gym and a gate. I walked toward the gate, looking frantically for Jack and Gary. There they were, waiting for me. This was the best sight of the day.

In Rolla, I valued my independence and enjoyed walking home alone, trying to find new routes. Now my brothers were my life raft, my security on a turbulent sea. For the first time that day my heart stopped pounding and I relaxed. I smiled and ran to them as we started to walk home.

"I am so glad I found you. I don't know how to get home."

Jack said, "We came from that direction. Follow me and I think we turn left up here."

"How was it, Gary?" I asked.

"Awful! This school is so big and we kept changing classes and teachers."

"Me, too! I don't know how to get anywhere. This is so scary. I don't like it."

"I don't either, Gong!"

We got to Foster Road and turned left toward home. There were no sidewalks along the road, so we walked single file while watching out for cars. Soon we reached the IGA store and walked down our driveway to our house. It would all be fine now.

Mom stood at the door to greet us. "How was the new school?"

We were all quiet. Then Jack said, "It was okay. Just big!"

Gary said, "We had to keep changing classes and I had three different teachers."

Mom looked at me and I said, "It was awful. All the kids were staring at me. Everyone already has a friend. I was always lost in that big school."

Mom's education had been in a one-room schoolhouse, where she arrived each day with her siblings transported by a team of horses. How could she relate to this?

Then Jack said, "Hey, let's watch TV."

We raced to the living room, forgetting our troubles. There was a show on called *The Mickey Mouse Club*. Soon we were engrossed in the adventures of Annette and Mickey Mouse cartoons.

By Friday of the first week, we were all becoming acclimated to this chaotic school. I was overwhelmed and had become that shy little girl that Grandpa Johnson liked to tease and call Silence. The kids were nice but preoccupied with their group of friends, while I remained mostly silent during the day. I had left the cocoon that gave me such confidence in Rolla, but my butterfly self wasn't ready to emerge.

Mrs. Flanagan's class had sharing every Friday. This was new to me, too. She would call on kids to show a toy they had brought from home, or they could talk about an experience they had. It was voluntary. If you wanted to participate, you raised your hand and when called, went to the front of the room to talk. I was mortified. I could never do that! I sat at my desk and listened and enjoyed the kids' stories.

After a couple of weeks, Mrs. Flanagan came by my desk and asked me if I would like to participate in sharing that Friday. My eyes got big and I replied, "No."

There was no way.

Then she said, "We would all like to hear from you Kathleen. So, think about it and maybe you'll change your mind."

She patted my head and smiled. I really liked her. She was so nice, but I wouldn't change my mind.

At recess, I continued to stand by the pole, helping it hold up the roof of the patio as I watched my classmates jump rope to different chants. I now knew who the experts were, and I was also learning the rhymes.

Once again, Mrs. Flanagan approached me and said I could jump rope, too. I didn't want to tell her I didn't know how, so I just told her I didn't want to. She patted my head again and walked on.

The first week we arrived in Portland, Dad checked on his photography job but was told the position would not be filled. The studio had hoped to expand, but business was just not good enough at that time.

Mom and Dad had to decide what they would do next. Both felt that this house might be just a temporary stop, so the boxes of items we didn't need for daily living were still packed and sitting around the living room.

Mom and Dad met with real estate people during the day while we were in school. Dad had decided that he wanted to run a bar or night club. He believed that selling liquor in Oregon would be a profitable move.

As Jack, Gary, and I walked home from school each day we reminisced about life in Rolla. As soon as we got home, we turned on the television. We were only half-listening to their discussions as Mom and Dad tried to figure out our next move.

One afternoon, I decided to make a dress for my doll. Mom had unpacked some pieces of fabric and I set about creating a small dress. When it came time for fasteners, I found her round metal button box, which contained a large assortment of buttons from some of her sewing projects and buttons that we cut off of worn out clothes. We always saved every button.

I searched through the box and found four very small mother-of-pearl buttons perfect for my project. I laid them out on the floor and got the needle and thread to sew them on. Nancy walked over to inspect the buttons. I told her not to pick them up.

Then I said something like "...and you don't want to put these little things up your nose."

I turned my back for just a minute, and Nancy picked one up and shoved it up her nose. I couldn't believe it. Then she started to cry as she put her little finger in her nose and pushed it farther up.

I called Mother. "I told Nancy not to put these buttons up her nose and she jammed one up her nostril."

Mother picked Nancy up and put her head back to so she could see the button and yes, she could, way up Nancy's nostril.

"Why did you say that, Kathleen? You know that saying 'Don't put this up your nose' just put the idea in her head."

Nancy continued to cry, and Mother's frustration only got worse. "How can we get this out! Gong, I expect more of you than this!"

She was really angry now!

"What are we going to do? I have no idea where to take her for help! I am very disgusted with you, Kathleen!"

I put my head down and started to cry. *Why did I say that? What was I thinking?* The guilt was too much. *What if they couldn't get the button out? What if it lodged in the part of her brain where you learn to read and she could never read? What had I done to my sister?* Dad came in and Mom told him what an idiot I was. He didn't say a word, but he gave me "the look" that made me feel like I was not worthy of living.

His answer was, "Call Elsie and find out where we can take her."

In a few minutes, Mom returned with directions to an emergency room nearby. They grabbed Nancy and left.

Jack and Gary were watching TV, and I was in the "gasp for breath" stage of recovery from a good cry.

Gary said, "Well, you didn't tell her to put them up her nose."

Jack added, "Little kids do stupid things. You can't give them the idea or they'll do it."

As I took a deep breath, I decided the only answer was prayer. I walked to the corner of the room and softly said:

> Dear God. I need your help now! My sister may be dying of Button Brain right now. I am in big trouble. I didn't plan this. Sometimes things just come out of my mouth without me thinking. Please help me! Make Nancy OK. I will try very hard to be a better person.
>
> Your friend,
> Kathleen

I didn't know what else to do. Suddenly, Mark was tugging at my skirt. He wanted a drink, so I took him into the kitchen to get him a glass of milk. I heard our car in the driveway. *That didn't take long.* In walked Mom, holding Nancy, with a big smile on her face.

Dad followed, and he looked happier, too.

Mom said, "We were on our way to the hospital, and Nancy sneezed and the button came flying out!"

Nancy was laughing. Mom and Dad took their coats off and began to relax.

Mom came out to the kitchen and said, "That was very scary. Kathleen. We were so worried about Nancy and we don't know where anything is in this town and we don't need a medical expense when Dad isn't working. I know you didn't mean to hurt Nancy."

It was a miracle! All I could think was, *Thank you, God, for creating that sneeze. It was a miracle. I am forever indebted to you!*

That was proof. Prayer did work.

Each night when we were in our bunk beds, we all reminisced about our previous life. Jack missed Rolla sporting events. We liked going to a school that included all twelve grades. We all knew the high school upper classmen that were on the basketball team, and we knew how our team, the Bulldogs, were faring against other teams in the area.

Gary talked about the times he played with Bobby Dunlop, and I missed Janice terribly. The bewilderment and isolation that we felt in this new school was offset by sharing the difficulties we experienced during the day, mixed with some of our fondest North Dakota memories. We were bonding as never before. It was us against a new community, and we were a team.

19.

On the Move

Mehama, Oregon
1956

"Strength shows not only in the ability to persist, but the ability to start over." —Unknown

Just two months after arriving in Portland, the boys and I walked home from school to find our truck parked next to the door of the house. As we entered, Mom and Dad were packing. We were moving again. The folks had talked to the Gilbert School principal that morning, and she promoted all of us to the next grade. We would miss the last month of school, but they all agreed it would be silly to start a new school for such a short time. We couldn't believe our good fortune.

We had all done well in our classes, but even after I quit wearing my long brown stockings and the boys gave up their corduroy shirts, we were always on the outside looking in. The drastic change in schools and community left us all in a bit of a daze. Jack was still recuperating, so his energy was not back to normal yet. We had been told by several kids that we had an accent.

If you've seen the movie Fargo, you have some idea of the North Dakota accent, even though the movie did exaggerate it. Living so close to the Canadian border, we apparently pronounced some words more like a Canadian. I had heard I said "aboot" rather than about, even though I was sure I didn't.

The rhythm of our speech was also slightly different. We ate breakfast, dinner, and supper. They ate breakfast, lunch, and dinner. We had never experienced the feeling of being different, and we didn't like it.

No one knew our grandparents or our parents. No one called from the Oregonian newspaper to ask if we had gone to Grandma's for the weekend. No one knew who we were, and no one cared. Like a distance runner completing a race, we all breathed a sigh of relief at the thought of leaving Portland. We were going to a new town; with summer days ahead, maybe we could adjust to Oregon after all.

The folks had purchased The Riverview Cafe and Lounge in Mehama, Oregon, a town seventy miles southeast of Portland with a population of about two hundred. Since Ernie and Herman had left for Rolla right after we arrived in Portland, we were on our own for this move.

Mom had our Norwegian trunk packed using every inch of space it provided. Our truck needed to carry the items that were initially transported in Herman's pickup in addition to the new furniture Mom and Dad had purchased. By the time the truck was packed, it looked like we were characters right out of *The Grapes of Wrath*, with items hanging on wherever they would fit.

Mom needed to drive the car for this move. She was very nervous about the traffic in Portland, but there was no other solution. When we were ready to go, Jack rode in the truck with Dad, and the rest of us climbed into the car as Mom followed the truck on our short journey.

About twenty miles from Portland, the highway went through Oregon City, a town famous for its steep hills. We all held our breath as Dad's bulging truck negotiated the roller-coaster route through town. Mom clung to the steering wheel as if it were a life preserver, and maybe it was. We were all silent, feeling the tension and not making a sound.

When we left Oregon City, we passed through a number of smaller towns where the driving got easier for Mom. With each mile that took us away from Portland, we all began to relax. The roads weren't crowded, it was a lovely spring day, and we were enjoying the countryside. The lush green vegetation and the tall, stately fir trees along the way reminded us that we were a long way from the North Dakota plains.

We turned right at The Gingerbread House, an ice cream shop located on the corner of the highway at the entrance to Mehama. It was decorated with blue, yellow, and orange wooden flowers on a chocolate brown building, and it advertised treats that made our mouth water.

We continued for one more block and turned left at the long rectangular building with a door in the middle and a sign on the roof announcing the *Riverview Cafe and Lounge, Chinese and American Food*. Dad drove around to the back and parked as close as he could to a small white clapboard house near the river bank. Mom parked beside the truck, and we all jumped out to hear the roar of the river in this tiny, sleepy town.

We walked to the edge of the yard and looked down through trees and shrubs to see the edge of the river and the whitecaps of the rapids, as the Santiam River moved swiftly under the green metal bridge at the end of our property. The view room of the restaurant's lounge faced the river. A log truck with five enormous logs was just crossing the bridge. The clean, clear water that recently was part of the snow-capped mountains nearby sparkled in the sunlight as the river surged on.

Dad opened the door to the house, and we all followed into the small, dank cabin-like building. It smelled musty, with traces of soot and ash from the fireplace. The kitchen had a window facing the river. The living room had a larger window focusing on the view. A floor-to-ceiling stone fireplace filled the wall across the room. There were two small bedrooms, and a bathroom with a toilet, sink and tub. Mom and Dad took the room to the left, and we had the one to the right.

The priority was to get boxes moved in and the beds set up for the night. With some work, this could be a comfortable home. It was small, but we had done small before, so we all started hauling boxes into our new home.

Mom and Dad's double bed and dresser took up their entire room. The two sets of bunk beds were set up in our room with just a walkway between them. There was no room for Nancy's crib, so she slept with Mom and Dad that first night.

The next day, Dad moved his saw and a few other tools into the cluttered, dusty shed just across from the house. He made a frame that held Nancy's crib mattress and fastened it on the wall above their bed. If she fell, she would have a short drop onto their quilts.

Soon it began to feel like home. After the television was installed, we found that we got just one channel instead of the three we had in Portland, but at least we had a television with reception.

Later that afternoon, Dad took us on a tour of the empty café. As we entered through the back door, we were in a sizable kitchen with an enormous range, a walk-in freezer with a massive metal door, and a couple of large islands for food preparation.

The property had been unoccupied for a while, and the stillness of the empty building combined with the coolness of this room made me shiver. I had a lonely feeling as I inspected our new acquisition. It reminded me of our store after the inventory and fixtures were removed. The building had became lifeless.

A door led into the restaurant. There was a long counter with stools needing customers. Four Formica-covered tables with chrome legs, so popular in the fifties, completed the room. One was gray, one red, one pale green, and one yellow. Each table had six matching plastic-covered chairs.

A door in the middle of the building led from the restaurant into the lounge. To the left was the bar, with more stools and a counter. The wall behind the bar was covered with mirrors and shelves that held decorative bottles of liquor. On the right side of the door was a large jukebox. Dad plugged it in, and multi-colored lights flashed through plastic panels on each side. The glass-covered top enclosed a record player with an arm that woke up when it was paid. Dad put a dime in the slot and selected a song from the list just beneath the record player. The sound of Gogi Grant's voice singing "The Wayward Wind" filled the room from the surrounding speakers. We were spellbound. Our often-used record player was nothing like this. The jukebox made the room come alive!

Across the spacious wooden dance floor huge windows framed those lush Oregon trees. Customers could enjoy cocktails and dinner in the red imitation leather booths while dancing to their favorite tunes and enjoying the Oregon scenery.

The riverbank beside our house was steep and covered with wild vegetation, so there was no easy access to the river. The main road through town ran beside our cafe and then onto the green, steel-framed bridge. The Bridge Tavern, located directly across the road from the Riverview, was our only competition in Mehama. It just sold beer and closed earlier than our lounge.

Often Mom and Dad's busiest hours were when loggers and mill workers left the tavern and crossed the street to our place. The Riverview was open from four in the afternoon until two-thirty in the morning. Mom and Dad had no restaurant or bar experience, but they were eager to learn.

Dad said, "There is quite a profit to be made with each alcoholic drink you sell."

We hoped so. The plan was that Dad would be the manager and the bartender. Mom would do the bookkeeping and be a back-up waitress, filling in during rush times. Dad hired Dale, a professional cook who moved to Mehama with his wife and stayed across the street in the Bridge Motel.

Dad drove to Salem to purchase liquor and to put The Riverview on food delivery truck routes. A Mayflower milk truck, Franz bread truck, and Boyd's coffee truck, among others, soon found their way to the back of the restaurant, and the drivers became our new friends.

The restaurant opening was not spectacular, and the place was not jammed with hungry appetites. This was a small community, and the restaurant was not on a huge thoroughfare. It didn't take long for the folks to realize that a professional cook was overkill for this operation. In just two months, Dad had to let Dale and his wife go, replacing them with a local cook.

The lounge was showing profits, but the restaurant was draining those funds. To minimize expenses, Dad also started assisting the cook during dinner hours. Mom became a waitress and part-time bartender.

This meant that we were unsupervised from four o'clock on. When Mom and Dad went to the restaurant to work each afternoon, we took over caring for Mark and Nancy, always aware that we lived by a river. We needed to ensure they were not venturing beyond the edge of our yard.

Log trucks flew through town right in front of our restaurant on their way to the mill in Lyons, a small town just seven miles away. The river and the road in front of the café were dangerous for a two- and four-year-old, so our job was to keep them safe. Mark and Nancy would ride their trikes on the gravel driveway that extended from the front of the café to the house. When they really got their pedals going, we corralled them back to the house.

At dinner time, we would all go to the restaurant, sit up at the counter, and order our meal. Then we would return to the house and watch television or play board games. Mom tried to come home at bedtime, but if the restaurant was busy, she couldn't leave, so we got the little kids ready for bed and then got ourselves into bed each night. After closing up the bar, Mom and Dad returned home at about three o'clock each morning.

They came home exhausted. Mom had some serious varicose veins in her legs, and standing through her shift was difficult.

Their nights were always short, as the noise of five of us getting up each morning in that small house made sleep impossible. Mom seemed to soldier through this, but Dad's disposition changed during that summer, as it became clear that the restaurant was not doing well and that our family life was almost nonexistent. He became quiet and dismissive.

Jack and Gary were tasked with cleaning the restaurant and lounge floors each day. They often had trouble meeting Dad's standards. Dad's ulcer was acting up, and he was impatient with our antics. He started smoking, a habit he had picked up during the war, but later gave up. Spending each night in a bar serving many smokers, Dad joined in.

One morning he came out of the bathroom clean-shaven. We were out playing in the yard when Gary came out of the house and said, "Guess what? Dad shaved his mustache."

We were not used to seeing him without a mustache.

"No mustache?" Jack asked. "Gosh! He is really changing. Is he still a grouch?"

"Yes! He's still grumpy, and now he doesn't even look like Dad!"

During these days, we would sit on the lawn and reminisce about Rolla.

"Remember how much fun we had with Dean and Betty at Pearl's farm?" Jack would start.

"I remember once when we were there, they had this big, mean bull in a pen." I said, "I asked Dean why they had such a nasty animal on their farm. He just smiled and said, 'Go ask your mom about the birds and the bees.' I never did know what he meant."

"Did you ask Mom?" asked Gary.

"I did."

"What did she say?" asked Jack.

"She said, 'We'll talk about it later,' and then she walked away."

I was nine now. What would the rest of the summer bring? What would our new school be like? So far, Oregon had been pretty disappointing. It had to get better.

The Riverview Café and Lounge

20.

Here We Go Again

Mehama, Oregon
1956

"For what it's worth: It's never too late… to be whatever you want to be. …I hope you have a life you're proud of. If you find that you're not, I hope you have the courage to start over." —Eric Roth

"You missed that corner again! How many times do I have to tell you that the floor has to be clean each day? That means each corner. You seem to want to slop through this job and you can both do better. I get damn tired of repeating this every day. I don't know what you azzholes are thinking!"

When Dad was agitated his pronunciation sometimes reverted back to his early years when his family spoke Norwegian; somehow assholes became azzholes. Finished with his evaluation, Dad left the lounge and returned to the kitchen to continue preparation for opening the restaurant at four o'clock.

It was July and we were well into our summer routine. Each morning, we retrieved Nancy from her wall bed and closed the folks' door to let them sleep a little longer. We usually had cereal for breakfast. A grassy area extending from the side of our house to the road in front of the café was our play area. We often created villages and roads for our toy cars in a shady area under some trees encircled by our dirt driveway. Jack, Gary, and I played and kept an eye on Mark and Nancy as they rode their trikes around the circular path of the driveway.

When Mom and Dad got up, they took over caring for Mark and Nancy. Jack, Gary, and I tried to take advantage of living in this beautiful area and put a little space between us and Dad. I rode my bike all over town, which was essentially one main road. About a block from our café Ken Golliet's store sold groceries, household items, a few toys, and fishing supplies.

The post office was located a few blocks down the road, and my task each day was to pick up the mail. The postmaster and his wife became my friends, and they would periodically come to our restaurant for dinner. My favorite days were when we got a letter from Grandma Johnson or one of Mom's sisters. They all corresponded pretty regularly, so the entire North Dakota family was updated on our adventures.

Long-distance phone calls were expensive and reserved only for emergencies. Letters were the only means of communicating. Once a week the *Turtle Mountain Star* arrived, and as I handed my mom the paper, she would stop what she was doing in the house and sit down and savor every detail of life in Rolla.

Jack and Gary both liked basketball, so they decided to make a hoop and backboard. They hammered together a backboard out of wood scraps they found in the shed and were trying to attach a peach basket to it when their efforts caught Dad's attention. He agreed that this was a worthy project, so he got some plywood for the backboard and a post to attach it to. Then he and Gary drove to Lyons to purchase a basketball and a hoop.

As Dad was paying the clerk he exclaimed, "That's a heck of a price for a basketball hoop!" and frowned as they left the store.

Once home, he completed the project and began demonstrating how the game was played. As he jumped to shoot a basket, he landed wrong and sprained his ankle. We all shuddered as he limped to the house. This was not Dad's summer.

Our summer days were interrupted by the restaurant supply delivery trucks that drove to the back of the restaurant throughout the week. Earl Phipps drove the Mayflower dairy truck and timed his deliveries around his lunch break. With fishing rod in hand, he would walk to the bridge and fish. Jack was interested in fishing, so Earl taught him how to put salmon eggs on a hook and how to use a spinning reel to catch fish. Jack spent many peaceful hours fishing off the bridge that summer.

The family with Earl Phipps behind our café.

There was a small church a couple blocks from the house. On Sundays, Jack, Gary, and I would often go to Sunday School, as we were eager to meet other children. The minister took the older kids on a camping trip each summer, and that was a highlight for Jack and Gary.

Maybe the boys found out about Convict's Swimming Hole from our minister. That summer when the days were warm and a dip in the river seemed most inviting, they walked some distance down a country road to a swimming hole. The swift river rushing by our house was not accessible, and the current was too strong for swimming.

One warm afternoon, they invited me to join them. We climbed the slope in back of our shed and walked to a road above our house. Eventually we came to a fence, and lifting the barbed wire, we slipped into a farmer's pasture. We walked down a twisting path and through some trees to Convict's Swimming Hole. A giant rock stood in the middle of the crystal clear river, where, according to local lore, a couple of escaped prisoners temporarily hid to avoid capture.

A rocky beach bordered the river and a calm area in front of us stretched to the massive boulder. Water rushed by its opposite side, creating whitecaps as it churned in the main river channel. The water closest to the rock was a dark, blackish-blue, emphasizing the depth of the water. Closer to shore, as the sun filtered through the overhanging trees, the water was a pristine emerald green.

Older kids challenged each other to swim to the edge of the rock, demonstrating their courage in surviving the bottomless hole. I watched Jack and Gary rush into the icy water. At first, they were shivering, but then they relished the cold water, a stark contrast to our hot and sweaty walk. Once I got used to the water, I waded close to shore.

When it was time for a break, Jack came over and said, "You need to learn to swim, Gong. It's no fun just wading here on the edge of the water."

"We can teach you to swim. Then we'll all have fun," Gary chimed in.

Suddenly my learning to swim had become the summer project, and the boys worked with me each time we went to the swimming hole. They gave me tasks to practice and then would leave and swim in the deeper water. I'd sputter and spout and work on my assignments.

"Put your arms straight out in front of you with your hands together. Put your head face down between your arms. Now push off and glide," instructed Jack.

I had always been fearful of the water and didn't like to put my face under, but after several sessions, to my surprise, they taught me to dog paddle. I couldn't swim to the big rock, but I could paddle up and down close to the beach. They were right. This was a lot more fun.

We returned home to share the good news with the folks. Gary ran ahead and proudly said, "Mom, we taught Gong to swim!"

Mom smiled and was pleased with the news. She said we could all go to Convict's on their next day off. Elsie and Harry would be visiting from Portland that day and this would be a real treat. The café was closed on Mondays, our favorite days because the folks were home all day and night.

Mom decided we would take a picnic lunch and drive to the swimming hole to enjoy the water and the shade. When we arrived at Convict's, Mother was aghast at the size of the rock and the depth of the water near the rock.

"Oh my God! Is this your swimming hole?" she gasped. "The water by the rock is very deep. Thank God you didn't drown here!"

She couldn't believe we had been swimming in such a dangerous swimming area totally unsupervised.

"Gary, lock the door. Here comes Jack!" I commanded as Gary and I raced to the house to get away from Jack.

Jack, Gary, and I usually played together well, but we were normal kids. Some days, Gary and I disagreed with Jack and banded together in a pact to ignore him. Other times the mix changed and another unfortunate was on the outs. Once in a while someone got clobbered, and I remember a few bloody noses. We were kids and we were unsupervised. Usually, though, we put our differences aside as we tried to help each other take care of Mark and Nancy.

One day when we were walking home from swimming, Jack said, "Oh no! I'm getting a bad headache. We need to get home fast."

"Is it like one you had in Fargo?" I asked.

"It's bad," was all Jack said as we hurried home.

Once we got home, we told Mom and she got her usual remedies to help Jack: Vicks VapoRub on his forehead, damp towel over his eyes, and an aspirin with water. Then off to bed in our darkened room.

"Gong and Gary, you keep an eye on Jack. I need to open the restaurant. Watch Mark and Nancy."

With that she was off to start another shift at the café.

Unfortunately, Jack had a few more headaches, and since there were no medical facilities in Mehama, Mom and Dad were very concerned that he might have another serious problem, so they took him to Doernbecher Children's Hospital in Portland for tests. Waiting for the results was agonizing. Once again, we lived miles from expert medical assistance. Was this a relapse of some sort?

Finally, they got the test results: Jack was suffering from migraine headaches, just like Mom. This news was a great relief, compared to what it could have been, but unfortunately Jack has been plagued with these headaches all of his life.

School started in September, which meant that Jack, Gary, and I got up at the sound of the alarm clock, ate cereal for breakfast, and walked a block to the bus stop. The school bus picked us up and drove us nine miles to Stayton. We were apprehensive about starting another new school, but we also missed having friends our age and were eager for the structure the classroom provided.

Stayton school was a long, rectangular building, with a straight hall and rows of classrooms on either side. Entering the front door, I turned and walked down the hall to the fourth-grade classroom. It was a rectangular room with windows along one side. Mr. Bates was my teacher. Our desks were set in five straight rows.

Starting a new school at the first of the year was easy compared to our experience in Portland. Getting to my classroom was simple. The bus was waiting for us by the front door of the school each afternoon, so I didn't give a thought to finding my way home. I had one teacher all day long and he was terrific. Soon, I had a best friend named Kay, and my desk was between Eddie and Darrel's. We were all good runners, so we ran all over the playground at recess and after lunch.

Gary was happy in his sixth-grade class. Mom and Dad decided that Jack should repeat eighth grade since he had missed so much school the previous year. He quickly found many friends in his new class and was selected to be on the basketball team. Everything was working out at this school.

The difficult part of the day was when we got home from school. As soon as we walked in the door, Mother was needed in the restaurant. She'd leave, and we'd monitor Mark and Nancy's activities and watch television until it was time to go to the restaurant for dinner. Then we returned home for the evening routine.

The days grew cooler as the Oregon winter set in. Heat for the house was provided by a stone fireplace. Firewood was piled out by the shed, and with the cool, rainy evenings we needed to make a fire each night. We took turns getting wood for the fire.

One of the disadvantages of living by the river was the river rats. These rodents were well-fed and at least a foot long. When we went to the woodpile to get wood for the fire, hiding under the logs would often be a fat rat with two eyes staring out at us.

One night, a rat made a quick jump to the ground and ran to the open door. I ran to the door and yelled, "Mark and Nancy, get up on the couch. There's a rat in here."

Jack and Gary grabbed a broom and a fireplace tool, and we all chased the rat back to the open door. This left my heart pounding. We were always cautious after we learned that the rats were much quicker than we were.

One morning our alarm went off and the three of us all went back to sleep. Obviously, we had stayed up too late the night before.

In a few minutes, Jack jerked awake and said, "We'll be late for the bus!"

We quickly dressed, grabbed some breakfast, and raced for the bus stop. We made it just as the bus approached.

Jack turned to me and said, "Gong, you forgot to comb your hair!"

I could feel my checks get warm as I looked in the reflection of the store window. My hair was a mess. *How could I be so stupid?* I tried to pat my hair into place, and Jack and Gary ran their fingers through the back, trying to make me look presentable. The bus pulled up to the curb and we all climbed on. I sat in the first vacant seat, ready to hear kids talk about my "just got out of bed look."

No one said anything, so either they had other children to taunt or my brothers missed their calling as beauticians. I got through the day but never forgot to comb my hair again.

One of the joys of riding the bus was meeting Bonnie. She lived by the post office, but I hadn't met her during the summer. I sat by her one day and she told me she was going to a Brownie Scout meeting at the church that afternoon. Her mother was the troop leader. She invited me to join her.

I had seen girls wearing brown dresses with brown felt beanie hats, but I wasn't sure what Brownies was all about. I told the boys to tell Mom I was going to the church for a Brownie meeting and I went with my new friend. The result was a real treat for me, as I met other girls close to my age.

Brownies was all about learning to help people. This fit with my helper mentality, and I was addicted.

I wanted a uniform, but the folks explained that the restaurant wasn't doing well and a uniform was too expensive. I could get the Brownie Scout Handbook, though. I devoured it.

I learned the salute, the handshake, the promise: *I promise to do my best to love God and my country to help other people every day, especially those at home.* The motto: *Be Prepared.*

We met every Wednesday, which became my favorite day. Brownies were family helpers, and I was already helping at home, so this validated that I was on the right path.

Soon each class began practicing for the school's Christmas program. My class would sing a Christmas song that was new to me called "Silver Bells." I thought it was the most beautiful song I had ever heard.

I don't recall how we got into Stayton the night of the performance. No doubt a friend's parent drove the three of us. I enjoyed each performance in the school's large auditorium, and when it was my classes' turn, Mr. Bates gave us each a silver aluminum bell to ring.

When we got back to the café after nine o'clock that night, Mom was sitting at a table with Mark and Nancy.

"Tell me all about the program," she said.

Each of us enthusiastically gave her a rundown. She listened intently, saying she was very proud of us and wished she could have seen the program.

The next morning at school, Mr. Bates complimented us on our fine performance the previous night. He asked if any parents had not been able to attend the show. My hand shot up, but then as I looked around the class, I slowly brought my hand down. I was the only one with my hand up. I knew my folks wanted to attend, and I really wished they could have been there. My embarrassment finally ended when the recess bell rang and I was on the playground racing with my friends.

It was now just days before Christmas. Dad seemed happier lately. He got us a small Christmas tree, which we all decorated enthusiastically. He grew a mustache again so he looked and acted more like his old self. We thought about our dismal Christmas last year, and were grateful Jack was healthy and we were all together.

As we were all admiring our tree, Dad said, "I have news. I know it's been hard having me and Mom working so many hours at the café. This move was a mistake. We've sold the restaurant and we will be moving right after Christmas. We're going to Salem. Since it's the capital, there are lots of civil service jobs there. Mom and I want to work during the day and be home with you at night. Salem is a nice sized town with medical facilities available when we need them. It even has a college in town."

We all sat in stunned silence. I didn't know what to think. Our home life would be so much better with the folks around at night. We wouldn't have to be in charge. The problem was, I loved my school. None of us could think of anything we didn't like about the Stayton school. I felt tired thinking of another move. This would be our fourth school in one year. What would another new school be like? I really didn't want to find out.

Just then Jack broke the silence by saying, "I don't want to go. I'm on the basketball team. We're practicing and we're pretty good. I really like the guys. I like my teacher."

Mom said, "There will be a team at your school in Salem, Jack. You'll make friends again. It's hard to think of moving again, but we are so fortunate the café sold. We have been very worried thinking we might not be able to sell this place."

Jack frowned and had tears in his eyes as he said, "Last year wasn't good and this year isn't turning out much better."

Mom said, "Let's focus on Christmas. You're healthy and we are here together. We'll think about the move later."

"Well, we can't think about it much later if we're moving right after Christmas."

The day after Christmas, Dad moved the truck up near the house. Mom opened the Norwegian trunk and it was time to pack up. None of us had any idea what the new year would bring. The only certainty was, we were on the move again.

21.
The Oldest Daughter
Salem, Oregon
1957

"The secret of change is to focus all your energy, not on fighting the old, but on building the new." —Dan Millman

Dad got into the packed truck with Gary by his side. Mom once again drove the car. Jack shared the front seat with her, while Mark, Nancy, and I filled the back.

The most consistent thing about the last year was change, and as soon as Christmas was over, we had all quickly fallen into the packing routine we knew so well. The restaurant venture had been a mistake all the way around, and Dad had withdrawn from us as he tried to figure out his next move.

Our house on Fifth Street.

It did take time. We lived in Mehama eight months, and for about seven of those months, Dad had wanted to leave. We were regrouping now. The move to Salem had to be better. A smile appeared on Dad's face when he saw the Riverview Café in his rearview mirror.

We arrived in Salem in less than an hour and were thrilled to drive by the Oregon State Capitol building topped by the golden lumberjack. It was impressive.

The size of the town was also encouraging. Salem had a population of about 45,000, somewhere in between the tiny Mehama and the impossibly large Portland.

The folks had rented a three-bedroom house on Fifth Street, and it was clearly the nicest house we had ever lived in. It stood on a street of well-cared-for older homes, with Mill Creek sloshing along about five houses down at the end of the street. Our street was lined with mature deciduous trees. We had sidewalks, and a single-car garage faced an alley at the rear of the property.

The white, wood-framed house had a front entry, with four steps connecting the sidewalk to the porch. It had a sawdust furnace in the full basement common to Oregonians, but new to us. A large portion of the basement was taken up by a sawdust storage bin. A couple of times a year a large truck arrived and blew sawdust in through one of the basement windows. For a couple of days after that the smell of fresh sawdust throughout the house was pretty nice.

The huge furnace had a metal hopper with sloping sides which fed sawdust to a burner and warmed the house via ductwork. Dad filled the hopper each morning and we would have heat until the hopper emptied. If the hopper wasn't refilled, the fire would go out and have to be restarted with newspaper and kindling. Heating the house this way was inexpensive since sawdust was readily available from mills in the area.

The windows on either side of the front door filled the house with light, reaching into the dining room with its built-in china cabinet. Hardwood floors extended throughout the house. In the rear was a large kitchen with a row of windows over the sink and a spacious counter area. The house had three bedrooms and two bathrooms. Stairs outside the kitchen took you up to an unfinished attic room with a low ceiling that was a perfect place for our prized Lionel train. Mom and Dad took the front bedroom. The boys had three beds in a row in their room. The end room was for me and Nancy. This was a huge step up from the cabin we left, and we were delighted.

We unpacked quickly because after New Year's we needed to be ready to start school again. I tried not to think of figuring out another school. I focused on the fact that Mom and Dad would be home with us and this house was lovely. It was a well-built, practical home. There was nothing fancy about it, but we had space, and it just felt good. Mr. and Mrs. Lucas were our next-door neighbors and also our landlords. They became our substitute grandparents.

All too soon it was time to go back to school. Gary and I would be attending Garfield Elementary School, an old, traditional square brick school built in 1909, and located on the edge of downtown Salem. Jack would go to Parrish Junior High, a few blocks in another direction from our house.

Gary and I started walking to school the day winter vacation ended. Mom and Dad must have registered us at the new school before we went, so on that first day, it was just the two of us trying to find our way again. We discussed life as we followed the sidewalk for several blocks and then turned toward our school. After walking and talking a few more blocks, we looked up to see Meier & Frank, a large department store.

"Oh no! This isn't it!" I said, panicked. "We're lost!"

We both turned around to see where we went wrong.

"Let's go this way," Gary said as we both started running back where we had come from.

We weren't excited about being the new kids in school again, but to be the new late kids to school would be horrible. We got back to where we had turned and ran a couple more blocks and saw the school. Arriving sweaty and red-faced, we found the office, and the school secretary walked us to our classrooms.

It was easy to find our way in this square building. We were both in opposite corner classrooms on the third floor. My new teacher, Mrs. Ackerson, introduced me to my twenty-five classmates, and we all stared at each other as she found a desk for me.

Gary and I were both well trained in our "new kid" role. We knew not to start this school wearing our North Dakota clothes. We both knew it would take a while to find a friend, especially this being midyear, but we had each other.

The playground was as square as the school, so I had no concerns about finding our way home. The gate we entered was front and center, and Gary was just across the hall from me now. I could relax.

Meanwhile, Mom and Dad's priority was to figure out the civil service system and turn in their applications for employment. There were no more thoughts of starting their own business. They had lost money on the restaurant and knew that owning their own business was a twenty-four-hour-a day experience. They hoped to find jobs that had a start and end time each day so they could recoup their losses and be home with the family.

What they found was that the system was large and slow. To apply for a job, they needed to get on the waiting list to take exams for each position they were applying for. Then they could interview for any open position when they were one of the top five candidates on the waiting list. They marked the calendar for test dates and settled into some quiet days at home with Mark and Nancy.

January and February flew by. School was going fine, but I really missed my Stayton friends. The week of Valentine's Day, my friend Kay from Stayton wrote and asked if I could spend the night at her house and visit school one day. I got Valentines for all of my Stayton friends, and Dad drove me to Stayton to spend the night with Kay's family and visit school. I had a great time.

By April, Mom and Dad had taken several tests and were on waiting lists for interviews. They were getting nervous about their continuing unemployment and our decreasing funds.

It was time for school report cards. I was excited since I had been doing well in class. I knew a good report card would put a smile on their faces. At the end of the day, Mrs.

Ackerson gave us each a large white envelope with our name written in near perfect penmanship.

I stayed after school to help clean up an art project and missed Gary, so I walked home alone, faster than usual since I had good news to share. When I was about halfway home, I couldn't stand it any longer. I opened the envelope and read the report. My heart pounded. The grading system was Excellent (E), Satisfactory(S), Needs Improvement (N).

I read my report card twice. This couldn't be happening. My report card had two N's. I couldn't believe it. I was so ashamed. Mom and Dad would be totally disappointed in me. My graded papers had all been good. How could I get two N's? I slowed my pace as I continued my walk home. I was no longer in a hurry.

When I got home, Mom and Dad were reviewing Gary's report card, which was very good. Now it was my turn. With tears in my eyes, I handed my progress report to my Dad. He read it and said, "Very good, Kathleen." I looked at him carefully and thought there must be something wrong with his eyes. Did he need glasses?

"Very good?" I asked. "I thought I was doing well and I got two N's. I've never gotten N's before."

Dad said, "Did you read the report?"

"No. I just saw the N's and wanted to cry!"

"Well, you have excellent marks in reading, spelling, and math, which are the subjects that count. In penmanship, you have an N, and the teacher commented that you do not form your letters to the Oregon standards. That means you came from another state that uses different penmanship standards. You'll get that right in no time. She also gave you an N in speech pronunciation. She says that you pronounce some words with a Canadian accent: Instead of saying "about," you say "aboot" and instead of saying "ant" for your mother's sister, you say "aunt," which rhymes with haunt. This is because we lived so close to Canada. This will also change when we live in Oregon a little longer. This is a very good report card."

Mrs. Ackerson's fourth grade class.

Wow! My dad was the best! I guess the N's were because we moved here from North Dakota. I needed to pay attention to how my new friends talked, but I didn't think I said "aboot."

With Dad's free time at home, he had painted the truck bright red and sold it. There was no good place to park it by our house. As we watched our truck be driven away by its new owner, I was glad that our moving days were behind us.

Dad was watching our budget very closely. He carefully read the grocery store ads in the newspaper each week, making lists and planning meals. He went to several stores each Friday, only purchasing the bargain items. Meanwhile, Mom was busy with the other household tasks and spending time with Mark and Nancy.

The folks' testing and interviews continued, but neither had a job. Dad mentioned often that there were lots of jobs he thought he could do, but a college degree was required.

Nancy's third birthday party with Mr. and Mrs. Lucas.

"Education is important," he'd frequently say. "Get a college degree and no one can take that away from you."

Dad had applied for several jobs that he didn't have experience for. Finally, he went to the Marion County Civil Service and applied to be a deputy sheriff. He had experience in law enforcement. That might be the answer.

One afternoon, when Mom brought the mail in, there was a letter from Grandma Johnson saying she and Grandpa were coming for a short visit. They were going to take the train and get out of the cold weather on the farm. They wouldn't stay long, as Grandpa was having heart issues and difficulty walking.

The Oldest Daughter

Mother started crying as she read Grandma's letter to us. Their upcoming visit was the best news she had had in a long time.

I don't remember a lot about their visit since we were in school all day, but it was wonderful for my mother to spend this time with her parents. Nancy remembers Grandpa walking around the block with her and Mark while they rode their trikes. Grandpa had a cane and had to stop midway and rest on a tree trunk before he could catch his breath and continue. Unfortunately, he would pass away the next year on the farm.

Grandma, however, was doing fine, and one day after school she stopped me as I was going to my room.

"Kathleen, you are the oldest daughter and that means you need to help your mother. You need to help with the cooking, the dishes, the laundry and the younger children. I was the oldest daughter so I know. I helped my mother all the time and excelled in my school work. I even helped build our sod house on the prairie. Your mother has had a difficult time with these moves. She has had those sick headaches since she was a child. She is very nervous. You must do more to help her."

I just nodded. Suddenly I yearned for an older sister like never before. Grandma walked away and cornered Jack, and I could hear her telling him that he needed to help more, too. I was a little taken aback because I felt like I already helped my mother a lot with Mark and Nancy. With the folks not working right now, we were doing less than we had at Mehama, but we all helped. I thought it was time for Grandma to go home. They left two days later.

Some days we came home and Dad had made donuts or cookies for us. It was nice having the folks home, but it was clear that we needed to have checks coming in because we were running out of money.

I wondered what I could do to help. I decided I needed to start praying for them to get work. We needed God's help and soon. We learned in Sunday school that God answers prayers, and I remembered the miracle of Nancy sneezing when I was so afraid she would have permanent button brain.

I began praying each night and finally, in late May, Mom got a notice that she had a job as a clerk typist. We rejoiced! She would start work on Monday. She wouldn't make a lot of money, but it was a start and she would be getting a regular check. She would try to get a better position using her accounting skills later.

Dad's cookie recipe

After a couple more weeks of praying, Dad got a notice that he would start work as a deputy sheriff in a couple of weeks. This was a huge relief.

Gary and I were cheering when I said, "It took a lot of praying, but it finally worked."

Gary looked surprised and said, "I've been praying for Dad to get a job, too!"

"That's it," I said. "We must both have to pray to get results. Maybe we didn't start praying soon enough."

It had taken a long time. The rules of religion were unclear, but if we kept trying, we knew we could figure them out.

In June, we were out of school and back in charge of taking care of Mark and Nancy. There were a few older kids on our block. There were a couple of high school girls that thought Jack was awfully cute.

On the other side of Mill Creek was the Miller home. Cheryl had been in my class and I liked her. The boys knew her older brothers, so we'd go over to their house and play kickball on their dead-end street. We created bases with chalk or rocks and enjoyed good times playing with our new friends.

Before Dad started working, he made a sandbox for Mark and Nancy and put it in the front of the house. They spent lots of time making castles and roads for their cars.

That summer, as they played in the sandbox, Gary and I sat on the porch watching them. One day a car stopped in front of our house and a man got out with a camera. He was from the *Statesman Journal* newspaper, Salem's finest, and asked if he could photograph them.

I had dressed Nancy in an old play suit of Jack's that I had found in the Norwegian trunk. I thought it was really cute, but I had no idea that the next day, on the front page of the paper, in a column called "The Brighter Side," Mark and Nancy would be featured playing in the sand. We were all thrilled when we saw the paper the next day. We were living with celebrities.

As I said, we all liked our house, but it was a rental. Mr. Lucas did not want to sell it.

Dad came home from work one day and said, "We're going to be moving again. Renting a house is just like throwing your money in the garbage. Buying a house is an investment. Mom and I are working with a real estate agent, and we're going to buy a house soon."

Why not? We had been in this house almost six months now. I couldn't believe my ears.

"Oh no!', I said. "Will we ever be home? I just want to have a home that isn't always changing!"

Jack said, "Buy a place in the same district so I don't have to leave Parrish."

Jack really liked his new school and was once again on the basketball team.

Gary said, "Well, whether we move or not, I'll have to go to a new school."

We could tell that Dad was serious, so we began mentally preparing for another move. Maybe our luck was changing.

22.

Buck Up, Buttercup

Salem, Oregon
1957

"Someday, everything will make perfect sense. So for now, laugh at the confusion, smile through the tears, be strong and keep reminding yourself that everything happens for a reason." —John Mayer

The search for a home with a maximum price of $10,000 resulted in two final choices in the Englewood School district, in the northeast part of Salem. Both houses were similar in age, size, and style.

The winning home stood at 1455 19th Street NE, across the street from a park, adjacent to Englewood Elementary School, my new school. I wasn't excited about another new school, but I knew it was always easier to change schools at the beginning of the year. Since we were buying a house, maybe our moves would be over. Jack was happy since he did not have to leave Parrish. Since Gary was entering seventh grade, he would be joining Jack.

Our new house was smaller than the last one. It was another square building with two front windows separated by an entry door. It had a few steps leading up to the front door.

Inside were a small living room, small kitchen, two bedrooms and a bathroom downstairs. Upstairs were a room with a couch left by the previous owner and a doorway that opened into a large, rectangular room that would hold the three boys' beds dormitory style. It had a small closet and little storage area on one side, with a couple of poles for hanging extra clothes, and under a small window, a space for our Norwegian trunk.

Mom and Dad took the front bedroom, and Nancy and I had the back bedroom, with a small bathroom in between. The back yard was large and fenced. The basement had an area for the washer and dryer, a work table and some tool storage for Dad, a space where he could build a darkroom, and some shelves to store canned food. A sawdust furnace and a sawdust storage area occupied a quarter of the basement space.

Our new home.

We were the only family in the neighborhood with a working mother. The folks made it clear to all of us that we needed to behave and cooperate with each other. We were certainly old enough to know how to behave. The boys needed to mow the lawn, and we all needed to help clean the house on Saturdays. No neighborhood children were allowed in the house during the day. I needed to take care of Mark and Nancy during the day. Certainly, the boys could help at times, but this decision played to my strength. I was good with this; don't forget, I was the oldest daughter.

Mom was employed in a typing pool for the State of Oregon. She sat in a room with about ten other women who each had a small desk with a typewriter on which they typed all day.

Mom really liked her boss, Edna Bartriff. The only phone in the office sat on Edna's desk. Mom was very serious when she said that if we had an emergency, we were to call her office. We certainly couldn't call Dad at the sheriff's office. The calls had to be only for genuine emergencies, and not because we weren't getting along. We needed to work together, figure out our disagreements, play in the park, and watch TV.

Living close to the park got us out of the house and the isolation of a back yard. By simply walking across the street, we would be welcomed by the tall fir trees of the seven-acre park and could quickly find other children congregating in the park ready to play. The boys left each morning with bats and balls in hand and spent hours playing baseball with other kids. The park had the obligatory swing sets, and a slide nestled deeper in the woods away from our house. There was an area closer to us that was open space bordered by a children's concrete wading pool.

I joined the boys on the weekends or when Mom and Dad got home from work. The open space became our ball field, and the lot for the team tag games pump-pump pull away and prisoner's base. It's where we became friends with the neighborhood kids. We were getting lots of exercise and really enjoying ourselves, but most importantly, learning team playing skills and getting through the day with kids in about a ten-year age range with no parental supervision.

Most of the players were boys, often led by my brother Jack since he was one of the oldest. I enjoyed playing with a couple of girls in the neighborhood, but it always seemed to me that the most fun was playing the games with the boys. Often, two of the older boys became team leaders for a game and chose teammates one at a time from the group.

I was always one of the last chosen, partly because of my age, partly because of my sex, and mostly because I wasn't that good. Still, it was great to be part of a team. Our leader defined a strategy for winning that seemed to work about half the time.

During the week days, Parks and Recreation employees hosted craft activities on picnic tables under the lofty trees, and each day, the wading pool was turned on in the afternoon. I would take Mark and Nancy, in their bathing suits, to the pool to enjoy the refreshing respite. Mark was five and Nancy was three that summer.

For an extra treat, I would pour milk into a quart jar, add some Nestle Quik chocolate mix, make peanut butter sandwiches, and grab a blanket so we could have a picnic in the park before their swim. They were always thrilled with this. Sometimes, we had graham crackers for dessert. I'd marvel at how easily entertained they were and I was rewarded with their enthusiasm for every small effort.

There were times, of course, when the days seemed long and I just wanted to play and not take care of children. I was happy to see Dad drive in the driveway a little after four each afternoon. We were expected to have the house picked up and breakfast and lunch dishes done for his arrival, which typically meant there was a mad scramble at 3:45 to get everything in order.

Dad would usually start dinner before picking up Mom, who got off at five o'clock each day. When they returned home, he would continue making dinner and she would take a load of wash to the basement. One of us would set the table, another would peel potatoes, and when dinner was ready, we would all listen to *The Huntley-Brinkley Report* as we ate.

After dinner, the park was a haven for Jack, Gary, and me. We would meet with the Snider kids, Johnny McKesson, Mike Yeager and others, and figure out what game to play. As the sky grew darker, we would often move to Virginia Street, a dead-end street that bordered the Sniders' house, and play Kick the Can.

As nine o'clock approached and it became difficult to see the can in the middle of the street, we would hear our mother opening the screen door of the house and yelling, "Jaa-ack, Gaa-ry, Go-ong!" and it was time to go home. About the same time, Mrs. Snider would open her door and blow a whistle, which her children knew meant that it was time to come in. The Snider children would run when they heard the whistle.

Mother often commented that the Snider children had a much quicker response than we did. They would run to their house and we would slowly amble home, tired from the busy day, but hating for the good times to be over.

Most days went well, but I still remember one hot, humid day when I couldn't wait for the folks to get home. Mark and Nancy were fighting over a golden book, and Nancy was crying as Mark pulled it out of her hand. She toddled to me for comfort, and I automatically picked her up. That day I was very tired of my adult role. We had celebrated my tenth birthday that May, and today I wanted to walk to the park alone and enjoy a moment of silence. I was having the housewife blues at age ten!

This time of day was always the hardest, as we were all hot, tired and hungry. I was spent. I had used my imagination all day to occupy them. How many stories had I read? How many drawings had we done? How many times had I pushed them on the swing?

Mom came in the house with a glow and burst of enthusiasm we didn't see often after her day at work. She put down her purse, grabbed Nancy, and told us she had a great story to tell us on the front steps. We all went outside and gathered around her. She held a piece of paper in her hand as if it were a treasure. She had been chosen by her boss to go to a special luncheon with selected employees from other departments to hear a guest speaker. This was a welcome change from the usual sandwich at her desk. I wanted her to get on with the story. How could her day have been so happy?

"So, what happened?" I asked as I grabbed the paper from her hand.

The paper tore in half, and I will never forget the horrified look on my mother's face. The guest speaker at her luncheon was the movie star, Jane Russell. The precious paper had Jane's autograph on it and now I had ruined it. I had hurt my mother, and tears rolled down my face as I took the two pieces of paper into the house and taped them together. I took it back to her and went into my bedroom and cried.

Later that night, after Mark and Nancy were in bed, Mother said, "I know some of the days are long for you, Gong. I like to see you go off and play with other kids in the evening."

Jane Russell's autograph.

"I just wish you could be home with us. All the other kids have their mothers at home." I sighed.

"I know, but remember just a few months ago when you were praying that we would get work. We finally did, and now we have to work hard to get back on our feet. I would like to stay home with all of you every day, but that is not going to happen. Dad and I can barely make it with both of us working. Remember, this house cost almost $10,000. That means a very large house payment. I am the only clerk typist that is over forty. This is an entry-level job and I am just happy to have it. I will move up to an accounting position someday, but until then, I spend all day typing. I get tired, too, and look forward to 5:00. We all have to work. This is just the way it is, and there is no need to talk about it. We can do this."

"I know. I just miss you." Mom patted me on the head and the discussion was over.

Buck up, Buttercup!

23.

The Longest Year

Salem, Oregon
1957-1958

"You call it chaos, we call it family." —Anonymous

The stately evergreens towered over me as I tramped through the park on my way to my new school. I had carefully ironed my red plaid dress. My brown leather buckle shoes were polished, and my pencils were sharpened and in their place in the green-and-blue box I had bought at Tindall's Pharmacy.

This was the first time I was starting a new school without my brothers, and I missed them. My stomach churned as I approached the huge brick three-story building peeking through the trees.

The air was crisp, with the hint of coolness of the approaching fall season. Pine needles carpeted the path, and sounds of children laughing and calling to one another after the summer hiatus filled the air. This was my fifth school in a year and a half, and I was now an experienced "new girl' in class, but right now it didn't seem to make it easier.

The previous summer, when Mark and Nancy were occupied during the day, I would think about going to another new school in September. I had heard a Ben Franklin quote on television that had stuck with me: "God helps those who help themselves." I was trying to figure out the rules of religion, and this was a new approach. Previously, I had followed the guidance given at Sunday School, that we needed to ask God for everything through prayer. I had tried that many times since we left Rolla.

Sometimes it did work, but it was very slow. When Mom and Dad were out of work, Gary and I had both prayed, and eventually our parents were employed. Did results require two people asking for the same thing? Were there a certain number of repetitions required? Was there a certain time of day that God was more available to listen? The rules were vague.

Ben Franklin was a wise and successful man. I decided to try to help myself. I knew not to let shyness overtake me. Withdrawing by standing and holding the patio cover up at recess like I had in the shell-shocked days of Gilbert

School wasn't a winning strategy. I couldn't sit back and expect the world to come to me. I needed to take charge. I was determined to make this fifth-grade year a good one, especially since Dad had sold the truck and maybe we weren't going to move again. I was ready to have a terrific school year.

I reached the asphalt-covered playground and saw a large easel on the side porch of the school with the heading Room Assignments. Kids were crowding around, searching for their names. I nervously looked for mine: Fifth grade, Kathleen Holstad, Mrs. Wharton, Room 15.

As I read the information, the words "Mrs. Wharton" slipped from my lips, and a tall, lanky boy beside me said, "Too bad! You have Warthog!"

He walked away with his buddy rejoicing in the fact that his teacher was Miss Hanna. A blond, pig-tailed girl beside me explained that "The Warden" was the worst.

"Is she really *that* bad?" I asked.

The answer was simple: "She's a witch!"

My shoulders slumped and the air went out of my first-day-of-school balloon.

"Where's Room 15?" I asked.

"I'll show you! I'm in Room 14 across the hall from you. My name's Brenda!"

We pushed through the heavy outer doors, and the aroma of freshly waxed floors, sharpened pencils, and chalk surrounded us as we climbed the wide brown-tiled stairs. Children were crowding the halls and searching the room numbers until they found their assigned class.

Room 15 stared at me as I opened the door and entered a large, rectangular room. Lights hung from the high ceiling on long cords. The wall opposite the door was filled with tall windows showing the tops of the trees in the distance. Single desks were pushed together to form a large "U" shape. The front of the room was covered with green chalkboards. The teacher's desk sat at the back of the room beside the near-empty cloak room.

I walked by each desk, several with students already seated, until I found the construction paper word "Kathleen" on a desk midway on the window side of the room. I sat down and took in my new surroundings. I liked the room. I had attended newer schools and older schools, and I liked this room.

The problem would be Mrs. Wharton. I carefully studied her amid the confusion of students entering the class, greeting each other, locating their desks, and sitting down. Mrs. Wharton was older than my mother, with lackluster black hair framing her face. Her skin was a dull olive color. Her back was rounded, shoulders slumped forward as she scanned the classroom and silently walked to the front. Mrs. Wharton's reputation preceded her, and as she stepped to the front of the class, her newly issued red attendance book in hand, we fell silent and all eyes focused on her.

Her severe voice was more like my father's than my mother's.

"I am Mrs. Wharton. This is fifth grade. When I call your name, raise your hand and say, "Present."

As she called names from Kevin Anderson to Steven Westfall, I examined the serious-looking faces of my thirty classmates and was glad we were all in this together. They didn't look like a bad lot, and it was evident that we had all heard the same stories about the "warthog." Now we would have to endure whatever that meant for a year. From the most serious student to the prospective class clown, we were all united in our wariness of the thick-armed woman dressed in the gold sweater and black skirt. We feared that at any moment she could go into a rage and cautiously waited for the other shoe to fall.

Suddenly, the speaker across the room exploded with a Sousa-like march, filling the room with a welcome distraction. As soon as I heard the sound, I wanted to laugh. The tenseness of the room had quickly changed to a gazebo-in-the-park atmosphere, and it was so sudden and startling that my first reaction was to laugh.

I was glad my brothers weren't in the room with me, as I know if we had made eye contact we would all have giggled. I had never been in a school with a sound system.

This was very high tech, but I was most happy for the diversion. The rest of the class took the sound box in stride. No one else seemed see the humor in any of this, so I quickly straightened up and told myself to be serious.

Next a xylophone pounded out three notes an octave apart: boom, higher boom, highest boom. The drama was killing me. Who in their right mind thought this up? Once again, the silent, expressionless class took it in stride as Mrs. Daugherty, the principal, welcomed us in a saccharine voice, the total opposite of our attendance taker. She explained that each week, certain sixth graders would read the news reports submitted by each class. Appropriate items like, the Smith family went water skiing at Devils Lake, were expected from students.

I cringed. Our weekends were spent at home, with Mother handing out various house-cleaning assignments to each of us. Then the folks got groceries, washed clothes, and decided which boy would mow the lawn. Mrs. Daugherty continued, saying that during this school year, each teacher would get to select one student for Student of the Week Award and that choice would be announced at the end of the weekly broadcast.

The day continued in an organized and serious manner, and soon the dismissal bell sounded. My brown leather shoes took me home through the park, now dim in the afternoon shadows. Our little house was a welcome sight after my new experiences of the day.

Mrs. Johnson, Mark and Nancy's elderly babysitter, gave me one of Dad's chocolate chip cookies on a paper napkin and a glass of milk as she asked about my day.

"It was pretty good," I said and let out a sigh of relief that the first day was over.

I knew it would be the worst: figuring out the new building, new friends, new books, a new teacher. The first three went well, but why did I get Warthog?

The cramped living room soon became cluttered with notebooks, books, and jackets as my brothers and Mom and Dad arrived home. The evening news anchors filled us in on the events of the day. Mark and Nancy insisted on coloring with the same crayon. Dad measured pancake flour and broke eggs for dinner, and Mom hauled laundry to the basement to start the wash.

Five hungry mouths suddenly appeared at the table, and as Chet Huntley and David Brinkley prattled on, we passed the syrup and filled up on Dad's thin, delicious pancakes with a cloudburst egg (fried egg with a soft yolk) on top. Five glasses of milk were filled, and then Jack and Gary had several more pancakes as Mom and Dad sat down.

During the commercials we shared the news of our day. I was abnormally quiet, still in shock about my distant and cold teacher.

After bathing Mark and Nancy, Mother appeared at my side as I dried the dishes. She needed pajamas for Nancy and sent me to fetch them from the dryer. Mom had already made the trek down the creaky basement stairs several times that evening and needed some help.

With three-year-old Nancy settled in front of the TV, Mother returned with the words "…and how was your day, Gong?"

Tears sneaked from my eyes and my first-day jitters suddenly dissolved in tears as I heard my busy mother's sympathetic voice. "Warthog" I blurted out. I had previously been emotionless as I studied my new surroundings, but now I could express my fears to my mother. All day I had a feeling of loneliness as I learned about the cafeteria, the bathrooms, the bell system, and yes, the public-address system with the square box on the wall.

I had hardly slept the night before as I anticipated the first day of school. New school, new books, new friends, new teacher, and I got Warthog! My mother listened, and my tears got her attention. I was her helper, the second mother for Mark and Nancy, so she noticed when I fell apart.

With the steam rising from the newly washed dishes I heard her say, "You can do this if anyone can. She may be strict, but she is probably a good teacher. Each day you'll know her better. Do the best you can and you'll be fine."

Right! What else could you do but deal with the hand you were dealt? The school playground was huge. Thankfully, there was was no rope jumping group in sight.

There was tetherball, which was new to me. There was Texas handball, or four-square, which I had played with my brothers. There were tennis courts with large rubber balls. There was a group of girls that loved horses and were running all over the playground.

I decided to try four-square and got in line. The girl in front of me turned and asked which classroom I was in.

"Mrs. Wharton," I replied.

She gave me a sympathetic look and introduced herself as Patty. We started talking as we each had a couple of turns playing the game until we were eliminated. Patty told me that the next day, she and her mother were going to a Girl Scout meeting. This really got my attention. Since I had just met her, I was shy, but I really wanted to be a Girl Scout.

"If it excites you and scares you at the same time, it might be a good thing to try." —Anonymous

Ben Franklin's words—"God helps those who help themselves"—resonated in my head as I said, "Last year I was a Brownie Scout and I really want to be a Girl Scout."

Patty thought for a moment and then said, "I think you're supposed to go to this meeting with your mother."

"Oh no! My mother works until 5:00 each day. What time is the meeting?"

"It's right after school at Pamela Davis' house."

I didn't know Pamela Davis, but I had to be a part of this. Taking a deep breath, I asked, "Could I go with you and your mother?"

Patty didn't know. She would ask her mom.

That night, as soon as my mother got home, I told her the big news. Maybe I could go to the meeting with Patty and her mother. Maybe I could be a Girl Scout.

The next day, I saw Patty on the playground before school and approached her. She had a big smile on her face and said her mother would pick us up at the front of the school and take us both to the meeting. I was thrilled.

Patty's mom, Mrs. Carter, pulled up to the school in her white-and-coral station wagon and drove us the six blocks to Pam's house. On the way, she asked about my family, when we had moved, and where we lived.

The Davis house was on a street with neat houses and pretty yards. Mrs. Davis was a beautiful woman with black, shiny hair and a perfect smile. The room was filled with girls and their mothers. I saw a few girls from my class.

We were divided into two groups. Patty and I would be in Mrs. Brady's troop. Mrs. Carter would be the assistant leader. Everyone got a sheet of paper with information on where to buy uniforms and the handbook, along with details about the meetings. This was fabulous!

I couldn't thank Mrs. Carter enough as she dropped me off at our house. When Mom got home, I quickly showed her the information. She read it and praised me for figuring out how to get to the meeting without her. She said we could go to Meier & Frank's that Saturday and get a *Girl Scout Handbook*, but the uniform would be too expensive to buy. The uniform would have been terrific, but I got to be a part of the troop. I was on cloud nine.

The next day Mom came home from work with an off-white wool coat.

"Marjorie sits next to me at work, and she invited me to go to a thrift shop with her over our lunch hour. My North Dakota coat is too heavy for Oregon, but I found this coat for three dollars. I'll have it cleaned and I'll be set."

That Saturday, I came in from playing outside in my last year's jacket and Mom said, "That jacket is just too small for you, Gong! I think I brought a jacket from the store that will fit you."

Mom and I went up to the Norwegian trunk, and she pulled out a red jacket from our store. Red was my favorite color, but my heart sank as I saw it. I knew our store well, and this was a boys hunting jacket. I tried it on and it did fit. It was totally plain with a zipper up the front and a small collar.

"But it's a boy's jacket," I said.

Mom just gave me "the look."

Christmas picture. Mark, Nancy, Gong in the red jacket.

I knew we were counting our pennies, but this jacket fit close around my hips and would look really strange if I had a full skirt on. It should be fine with my red plaid skirt, and maybe no one could tell it was a boy's jacket. I hoped we could get on our feet soon.

A couple of weeks later as the cool, rainy days were becoming more frequent, Dad said, "Kathleen, we need to have you help this winter. You will need to come home at lunch time each day to fill the furnace. I'll show you what you need to do."

This sounded important. Off we went down the stairs to the basement and our sawdust furnace. It was very similar to the one in our other house, but I hadn't paid much attention to it. Since Dad was home all winter waiting for a job, he had taken care of filling the furnace. Now I had to listen carefully and get this right.

About a quarter of the basement was taken up by the sawdust bin, which stood next to the large furnace. A metal hopper sat atop the furnace. Dad filled a bucket with sawdust and dumped it into the hopper. Then he set a five-gallon bucket upside-down next to the hopper and told me to fill the smaller bucket, stand on the larger bucket, and dump the sawdust into the hopper.

Okay, here I go. I filled the bucket, balanced myself on the five-gallon bucket, and dumped the sawdust over the rim of the hopper. Dad had me do this several times until the hopper was full. Then we got down on our knees and he showed me the burner. I could see the orange, flickering flame.

Dad said, "If the hopper is empty, the fire goes out. If that happens, you'll need to strike a match and light a newspaper from a pile in a box close by to start the burner."

By coming home from school during my noon hour each day, I could keep the fire going for Mark, Nancy, and Mrs. Johnson. Dad did not have time to get home on his lunch hour, Jack and Gary's school was too far away, and Mrs. Johnson was too old to do this. It would be my responsibility every day. I almost saluted. Yes, sir! I'm your man! I can do this. The new responsibility was heavy-duty. I could save the children from a cold house on the many rainy Oregon days.

Days became weeks and weeks became months. Mrs. Wharton proved to be strict, with never a glimmer of humor. Her classes were interesting, and I stayed busy. The classroom books were a treasure and assignments were many. The class was always under control. I was in the top reading group, and our stories and assignments were fun. The kids were nice.

Wednesday was my Girl Scout day, and I loved our meetings. I read the entire handbook the weekend I got it. The year was buzzing by.

I had a new awareness of the weather each day. Running home to fill the furnace on a windy, winter day was fine, but there were periods of seemingly constant rainy days when

I dreaded leaving the comfort of the classroom for my trek home.

I quickly learned that by running both ways, filling the furnace quickly, and eating lunch with some speed, I could be back to school for some of the lunchtime activities. Each day, Mrs. Johnson had my lunch ready when I arrived home. She had folded a napkin, made a sandwich, and put some of Mom's canned fruit in a little dish for dessert.

The worst days were when the furnace fire was out and I had to start it. If the sawdust was damp for some reason, the fire would go out or if the sawdust ran out before I got home, the flame would be gone. I dreaded those days, when nothing seemed to go smoothly and by the time the fire started burning, I had to run quickly in the rain to make it back to school.

On those days, I wasn't sure that responsibility was a good thing after all. It was the same feeling I had when I wanted my mother to have a baby. Babies were so cute and cuddly, but once we had them, we had to take care of them every day. It was constant. I liked being the helper and filling the furnace, but the problem was, it needed to be fed every day.

One dreary January day, Mrs. Wharton said, "Kathleen, why don't you bring your lunch on some of these rainy days. I'm going to have the class work on group projects after lunch when it is too rainy to go to the playground."

Suddenly I was embarrassed. I didn't want anyone to know that I had to fill the furnace.

I said, "Oh, I have to go home every day for lunch, but I could stay after school to work on a project."

"Well, we'll see. I often have appointments after school, but if you can't stay here for lunch, maybe you can do some project work at home."

It was time for the class elections for the second half of the year, and to my surprise, I was elected class treasurer. My heart leaped. We would be officers for the next four months. I felt accepted and was eager to do well with my new challenges. The treasurer's main responsibility was to sell saving bond stamps every Thursday.

The school savings stamp program had originated during World War II as a means of encouraging individual savings and to support the war effort. Now we were supporting the government and saving for a rainy day, and since this was Oregon, there were lots of those.

Students could fill a ten-cent stamp book with pink stamps or a twenty-five-cent stamp book with green stamps. After filling a stamp book, students could buy a savings bond that cost $18.75 and then redeem it after about eight years for $25.

My job was to pick up the Room 15 stamp envelope from the school office each Thursday morning and then, standing in front of the class, sell stamps to whoever wanted to buy them that week. I'd make change, fill out the form indicating money started with, number of stamps sold at ten cents and twenty-five cents, money received that week, and total number of stamps sold. Mrs. Wharton would check my math (we calculated everything using a pencil and paper in those days) and then I would take the stamp envelope back to the school secretary. This was an important job, and I took it very seriously.

The next Saturday, Dad went to Sears to get nails so he could put up more shelves in the basement. When he came home he had a package for me.

"I found this on a sale rack as I walked to the hardware department, Kathleen."

I opened the bag and found a blue, hooded jacket lined in white fleece. It had green, red, and yellow embroidery down the front. It was fabulous! I couldn't believe it. I tried it on and it fit.

"There was only one jacket like this on the clearance rack. You've been a real help this year, and I know you weren't thrilled about wearing a boy's jacket."

Wow! The jacket even had a hood. Bring on the rainy days, I was ready!

As spring approached, the weekly intercom broadcasts continued. We learned whose grandmother visited and which kids were working on Soap Box Derby cars.

On a dreary Oregon May day, Monday morning started like any other day. We sat in our seats, Mrs. Wharton had marked the red attendance book, and John Philip Sousa's music had filled the room. It was routine now, and my urge to laugh had come and gone.

I was half-listening to the fact the Sharon Weathers' father had gone on a trip to Chicago and that Beverly Marcroft's grandmother had visited from California when Mrs. Daugherty's voice announced the Student of the Week selection.

"This week's student is from Mrs. Wharton's class…"

It had to be Claudia. She was the smartest in the class and one of my friends.

"…The winner is a new student to our school that has done a fine job as classroom treasurer."

I didn't hear the rest. I was suddenly alert! Bells went off in my head, my heart was in my throat and then my stomach. How could this be?

"Would Kathleen Holstad please come to the office to pick up her award?"

In a semi-conscious daze, I flew from the classroom and floated down the stairs to Mrs. Daugherty's office. She patted me on the head and handed me the certificate. I couldn't believe it. The rest of that school day was a blur. Why would Mrs. Wharton select me? I needed to bring a picture of me to Mrs. Daugherty for the Student of the Week School Bulletin Board.

As soon as I reached our house that afternoon, I called Mom at work. The rule was not to disturb her at work unless it was an emergency. Well, this was an emergency! Mom's office phone rang, and her boss Edna answered.

"May I speak to Lyda, please?" I asked.

Mom's voice was higher that normal as she answered the phone, anxious to hear what had happened at home to merit a phone call, of course expecting the worst.

Student of the Week.

"I'm Student of the Week for the whole school," I blurted out.

The relief in Mom's voice was audible. She exhaled with relief and laughed.

"You were selected by Mrs. Warthog?" was her response.

I heard myself explaining, "She's not bad at all, Mom. In fact, she's really nice!"

I wish I could tell Mrs. Wharton what that award did for me. It wasn't the Pulitzer Prize or an Olympic Gold Medal, but to this ten-year-old girl, it was acceptance. There was a permanent shift in my brain that day. There were smarter people than me, better artists than me, faster runners than me, but for whatever reason, I could excel, too. It wasn't Rolla, North Dakota, but I had gotten to attend this school the entire year. I had found friends and activities, and I wasn't dwelling on what I had left behind. There was no time. I was busy with my new life. This might be home.

The school year continued and Mrs. Wharton's skin became more sallow. She seemed to walk slower, and I could tell she was ready for the school year to end. The year ended as it had begun, with no glimmer of amusement from our teacher. Get the work done, try hard, one foot in front of the other was the message all year. We received our report cards announcing our promotion to sixth grade. Summer was here, and not a moment too soon.

The next year Mrs. Wharton died of cancer. I was heartbroken when I heard the news. Without clicking her heels, she had fulfilled her teaching duties in a disciplined and thorough way. I had been hoping for a teacher who would be fun and enthusiastic, who would appreciate my antics and laugh as she gave me a few pats on the head.

That didn't happen. Instead, I had spent the year with someone that challenged me with interesting assignments and projects. She was a role model for a strong work ethic. She didn't need to be my friend, she needed to be my teacher. Through it all, she somehow had an appreciation for my efforts and gave me a boost that she must have sensed I needed. In the end, in her serious, stern way, she had really been my very best friend.

"All kids need is a little help, a little hope, and somebody that believes in them." —Earvin "Magic" Johnson

In December 1958, Dad set up his camera in our living room. He brought in the bright studio lights that had accompanied us on so many moves and had us pose for that year's Christmas card photo. Creating a card combined Dad's photographic and creative skill, and sent a message that he and Mom were proud of their family.

The Christmas card also represented the stability we were all feeling. The last card he had made was in 1954, at the end of a relatively calm period in our lives.

During the chaotic four years between cards, there was never a thought of sending a Christmas greeting to friends. There was no time to create one. Change kept happening, the folks kept busy, we kept moving, and we all wondered where it would end.

Christmas card, 1958.

24.

Make Lemonade

"If we know where we came from, we may better know where to go. If we know who we came from, we may better understand who we are." —Anonymous

It's been said that when life gives you lemons, make lemonade, and there is a wisdom in those words. The stories in this book speak of taking risks, falling down, getting up, having a strong work ethic, and the importance of family loyalty. They also illustrate the unpredictability of life. Try as we will to create a plan, life just takes over and suddenly we find ourselves on a different path.

In 1867, my great-grandparents, Mikkel and Martha Holstad, and their children, bravely stepped onto a ship with 250 other Norwegians, eventually ending up on a farm near Lake Mills, Iowa. Six years earlier they had married and probably never dreamed of traveling across the ocean to a new country. Their path had changed drastically, and the family had to work as a team to establish a farm, a home, and a respected place in the community.

Follow the Norwegian trunk and you go from Norway to Iowa to North Dakota and on to Oregon. Build a sod house on a prairie with the wind blowing, the grasshoppers invading, and the sun beating down. As a young woman, Grandma Johnson supported her parents as she lifted sod and helped create a house. Prepare for the harsh winter. It is coming. Work together. Support each other.

Art Johnson's father had a drinking problem that got in the way of his ability to support his family. As a fifth grader, my future grandfather Art quit school to earn money to help his mother pay the bills. There was a void, and he stepped up to the plate. The needs of his family came before his education.

Years later, Grandpa Johnson drove my mother to college with the dust from the fields covering their windshield and obliterating the roads. My mother graduated, gained employment in the Welfare Office, and paid the taxes on the farm when Grandpa couldn't. When my mother eventually decided to move to Oregon, Grandpa slipped much-needed money into her pocket.

We moved four times in 1956: different schools, unsettled homes, new friends, bewildered parents. We were confused children wistfully asking, "Is this home?"

Like newly hatched ducklings, we followed our parents' lead until we finally discovered home. We became different people from the innocents that began the journey. Now we knew that home wasn't a place or a building. It wasn't a basement house or a sheriff's house, or a house by the park. It wasn't large or small. Home was our family.

In 1958, our crazy years ended. After a couple of wrong turns, it seemed like we were getting it right. We had a real appreciation for our house on 19th Street and the fact that we were settled. We had a park across the street with neighborhood kids that liked to play ball as much as we did. Attending a school for a full year was a gift. Every day the folks got up and went to work. They got regular paychecks and we had medical benefits. We participated in school activities and made life-long friends. We had a working mother, so we all scrubbed floors, vacuumed, and took care of Mark and Nancy to pick up the slack.

While we were embracing our new life, a part of us still yearned for our North Dakota family. The folks remained employed in the civil service system until they retired. Each year they earned two weeks of vacation, and there was never any discussion about what we would do with that time. We eagerly packed the car and drove to North Dakota. Mom couldn't wait to see her family and we were all reunited with our cousins and old friends.

Higher education was a family goal, but my folks had no money to help us attend college. Instead, they insisted that we work to pay our expenses. The move to Oregon enabled all of us children to work in the fields during the summer, picking strawberries and beans, earning money to buy our school clothes. I even bought a Girl Scout uniform!

With the celebration of our sixteenth birthdays, we all got our work permits, joined the Teamsters Union, and became employees in various Salem canneries, saving money for future educational expenses. With the words of Grandpa Johnson and our parents ringing in our ears we all went to college. We were always able to support ourselves and, by the way, none of us ever bit the dog!

I mentioned a few chapters ago that when Grandma Johnson visited us in Oregon in 1957, she took me aside and described the role of the oldest daughter. I was offended at the time because I thought I was already doing my share, but her message was received.

Our parents had left the safety net of their North Dakota family. Life had given them a few lemons. They needed help to get back on their feet, and help must come from the children. As Grandma pointed out, that had been her role in the past, and as she passed the baton to me, I took it.

Now I'm the grandmother, and my simple message to my grandchildren is, continue the family tradition. The family is the first line of support in a sometimes unpredictable world. A commitment to one another is key. Help your parents. Look out for your siblings and cousins. Work together... and in the process, make some delicious lemonade!

25.

Epilogue

Escondido, California
2003

"Life doesn't come with a manual. It comes with a mother."
—Anonymous

Fast-forward 45 years from 1958, and my husband Carter and I are both retired and living on a small avocado/citrus acreage just outside of San Diego. Our two boys, Dave age 29 and Jeff age 24, are pretty well launched. They both live in San Diego and are employed as software engineers.

On a bright and sunny Friday morning in June, I dropped Carter and the boys off at the San Diego airport. They were eager to get on their flight and begin a five-day fishing adventure in Alaska. With hugs and kisses given and received, I pulled away from the curb and drove home. I was equally giddy about the next five days. I'm an avid quilter, and for several weeks I had been gathering gorgeous fabric for my long weekend reserved for creating an art quilt.

When I returned home, I went to my studio and began. I had no schedule. No meals to prepare at normal times. I could sleep in and sew until midnight. I had no one to consider but myself. Days like this were rare, and although I knew I would be lonesome by the time I picked up the guys at the airport, my adventure was about to begin. I measured, cut, and sewed the rest of that day and far into the night.

Sound sleep is a gift from the gods, and I was lost in a dream, when the bedside phone blared near my ear the next morning. I jerked awake and grabbed the phone, noting 6:47 on my digital clock.

With my heart pounding, I heard the voice of the director of my mother's independent retirement home, "Kathleen, it's Anne! Your mother is not doing well. She's feeling dizzy and is, at times, disoriented. She's afraid she will fall. I think you need to come."

"Okay, Anne. Tell her I'm on my way."

We had moved Mom into a retirement home a short time after Dad passed away in 1989. He fought the debilitating effects of ALS, or Lou Gehrig's Disease, until his death.

Mom and Dad had been married 49 years, and Mother really struggled with the void his death created in her life.

He had been her best friend for all those years, but she slowly adjusted to life in her home and for the last few years had really been enjoying several of the group activities.

I quickly dressed in my jeans and a T-shirt, ran a comb through my hair, grabbed a ball cap, and was out the door. It was three weeks until my mother's ninetieth birthday and we were hosting a three-day celebration for friends and relatives. Mother had no major health problems, just the wear and tear on a ninety-year-old body, which meant that lately she was having good days and, more frequently, bad days.

As I drove the forty-five minutes to her home, I mentally adjusted my expectations for my weekend. I would check out Mom's condition and go from there. As I turned off Gopher Canyon Road, the sun was shining and it was going to be another perfect day in paradise. There was almost no traffic and Roy Orbison was belting out "Pretty Woman" on my car stereo.

Anne met me at the lobby door. Fourth of July decorations abounded: Red, white, and blue stars and stripes were everywhere!

"I didn't think I needed to call the ambulance," Anne said, "but your mother is certainly not herself."

I knocked on mom's apartment door and said, "Liza May, how are you?"

Epilogue

Mother's name was Lyda May, but I often called her Liza May in my best Southern accent. It usually brought a smile from her. She was sitting in her wheelchair with a frown on her face.

"I am so glad you are here, Gong! I was so scared. I felt like I was going to faint."

She was almost in tears with her shrinking frame bent over in her chair. She looked frail and very old. My heart went out to her.

"Why don't you come home with me and you can rest and we'll watch movies, Girlfriend?"

She began to relax as I started packing her bag.

"Now I need my pillow and my Vicks," she said.

I knew this without her saying a word. Mother resorted to Vicks VapoRub for any medical problem. For a headache, rub some on your forehead. Sinus infection? Vicks on the forehead, warm towel over your head. Sore throat? Vicks on your throat and a man's sock pinned around your neck fastened with a large diaper pin. Cough? Vicks on the chest. She didn't go to sleep at night without Vicks up each nostril. This was her security. Sleep would follow as she breathed the comforting scent through her nose.

I finished her packing and was glad she had improved enough to give clear and firm directions. She needed to comb her hair and put on her lipstick.

"How do I look?" she asked.

I was making her bed and straightening up her room, and she was concerned about her appearance? That was my mom.

"Mom, you look great!" I said in an exasperated tone.

"You know, Gong, I would like you to take more care with your appearance. That baseball cap is not attractive!"

Mom and Gong.

Suddenly, I knew it was going to be a long weekend. I rolled my eyes, picked up her bag, helped her into her wheelchair, and pushed it out the door.

"Girlfriend, you already act like you're feeling better, "I said.

In response she directed, "Don't forget to take my walker, lock my door, and check me out with Anne."

"Yes, Mother!"

When we got in the car, she commented on the beautiful day. It was hard to ignore. She checked out the avocado groves as we zoomed by, and then her head dropped to her chest and she dozed off.

I had turned Roy off, as I knew the music would bother her. When she woke up, we drove in silence for a few minutes.

Then out of the blue she said, "You know, Gong, I couldn't have worked if you hadn't taken care of Mark and Nancy. What would we have done?"

Mom would bring this up fairly often lately as I drove her to various doctor's appointments. She seemed to be reliving some of the stressful times in her life.

"You took care of Mark and Nancy when I worked, but you were just a child yourself. I never thought how young you were. You were so responsible. What was I thinking?"

"It's fine, Mom," I said. "It all worked out."

She responded with one of her favorite phrases: "Well, I should say so!"

We were now buzzing down the freeway when she said, "I have a new vocabulary word."

Mother loved words. Once a week she attended "Fun with Words," an hour-long class at her home where residents learned definitions of new words and played word games. That and Bingo were her favorite activities. She would often call on Friday night to report in an enthusiastic voice that she had won $1.75 in Bingo that evening.

The highlight of her morning was the arrival of her newspaper, which she would quickly search to locate the crossword puzzle. Once she found it, she was lost to the world as she focused on each clue. She didn't relax until each square was filled with a letter. She often quizzed me on definitions of words.

"This week's word is galliot. Do you know what that means?"

"Not a clue, Mom."

"Well, a galliot is a Dutch fishing boat."

How had I survived fifty-six years without that knowledge?

"You really need to work on your vocabulary, Gong!"

She was back in her mother role again. I had recently retired from an executive position at Qualcomm and she was concerned about my vocabulary.

We arrived at my house, and I got her settled in the guest room and made her some coffee. Then I called my sister, Nancy, who lives about fifteen minutes away. She was very concerned about Mother and said she would be right over.

Nancy and Mother were best friends. My role was caregiver. I usually took care of Mother's needs during the week since I was retired and Nancy was still working. Often Mom and Nancy spent time together on the weekend going to dinner, shopping, and sometimes taking road trips. I was usually busy with my family and friends on the weekend, so our division of labor worked out well.

Nancy arrived in just a few minutes, having spent as little time on her appearance as I had. Mother noted this and we all had breakfast. Then Mother took her walker to her bedroom to rest.

Nancy and I were deep in conversation when Mother shouted, "Gong!"

She was frantic, and I raced into the bedroom to find her bent over the handles of her walker. I was standing behind her when she started to fall. She landed on top of me, with the walker on top of her. Her eyes were closed.

I yelled, "Mom! Mom!"

There was no answer. She had either fainted or was dead!

I yelled, "Nancy, call 911!" which she did immediately.

Meanwhile, Mother was still lying on me. I couldn't tell if she was breathing and I couldn't see her full face, but I could see that her eyes were closed. Her life flashed before me. One of six children born to North Dakota homesteaders, migraine headaches, and anxiety her entire life—always working full time, usually as an accountant, and then coming home and working far into the night to keep the family of seven going. My heart pounded like crazy again and tears slipped from my eyes.

In a flash, the paramedics arrived just as Mother came to. Four fit young men in navy blue uniforms entered the bedroom and lifted the walker off of Mother. Then I could ease her off of me as her eyes slowly opened. She was disoriented and confused.

The paramedics quickly determined that Mother probably had low sodium and low potassium, a condition they saw frequently in the elderly. She would need to be admitted to the hospital for IVs and observation. As they turned to pull the stretcher into the bedroom, Mom's color returned to her face. I was so relieved. This was not a serious condition.

Nancy grabbed Mom's suitcase and said she would go in the ambulance with her. I would follow in my car.

As Nancy squeezed by me, she whispered, "Four great-looking guys and I look like this."

I laughed. We had responded quickly to Mother's crisis that morning, but we could have at least taken a shower.

All of a sudden Mother grabbed my leg. I looked down at her and she said, "Gong, get my purse."

"Sure, we'll take your purse, Mom," I said.

"No, you don't understand. I need my purse now. I need to put on lipstick. Does my hair look alright?"

My mom was back. I found her lipstick, and she looked lovely as the paramedics rolled her into the ambulance.

Lyda May Holstad at ninety.

Mother rallied for her party and delighted in being the queen with her paper crown and her badge necklace which read "I am 90!" She enjoyed seeing all of the guests and, by the way, she looked terrific! Her white hair was soft around her face and she was glowing.

After the event, she slept for several days. She was totally exhausted, but kept all of her birthday cards by her bed and read them over and over again.

Two months later, Mother was sleeping most of the time. She was too tired for word activities and couldn't concentrate on Bingo. She was diagnosed with leukemia and passed away a few weeks later.

On one of my last visits to her 24-hour care unit, she had her eyes closed but was awake when I arrived. We talked for a few minutes. For the first time, I couldn't tell if she knew who I was.

I had to ask, "Do you know who I am?"

With eyes still closed, she replied with a smile, "Oh, I know who you are." She paused and then she said, "You are my girlfriend!"

Acknowledgments

Many amazing people helped me get this book into the hands of the publisher. I have to say THANK YOU in all caps to all of them. This book has certainly been a family/group effort.

Two years ago, my Saturdays were suddenly free because my grandsons were all old enough to participate in sports. We had shared great times together, but now they were moving on to team sports. I had wanted to document these stories, but I wasn't sure where to begin so I enrolled in a Memoir Class with Marni Freedman. I didn't enroll for the full package of classes because I didn't know Marni and if the teacher wasn't fabulous, I needed to move on. After the first class, I enrolled in all of Marni's memoir classes. She is a gifted teacher and she inspired and encouraged me all the way. Thank you, Marni.

The stories in this book took place over sixty years ago. As I was writing, I would check with my siblings for their memories of various events. Sometimes we all had very similar recollections and other times our versions were so different I wasn't sure we were all in the same family. We did have fun sharing lots of emails as we went down memory lane. Jack was a teenager when we left and he was key in recalling details and specifics of life in Rolla. Gary also provided facts and insights that added to the stories. Mark was three when we left, so a lot of this was new to him. Although Nancy was two when we left Rolla, she has great recall of stories Mom and Dad would tell about Rolla and our journey west. Thank you, siblings for all of your help.

Some of my cousins also contributed their memories of Grandma and Grandpa Johnson and life on their farm. Thank you, Dave Johnson, Linda Olson Tilton, and Alyce Ann Johnson Lunde. Linda also provided her mother, Ruth Olson's insights into life in North Dakota during the depression. Ruth has passed on so her story is a real treasure. Dean Thompson reminded me of Grandpa's greeting when we entered his house and that became the title for this book. Thank you all.

Thank you, Jason Nordmart for searching the *Turtle Mountain Star* archives for me. I appreciated Geoff Young's editorial skills and suggestions. Thanks Geoff.

Jack Holstad, Michelle Zhang and Alex Pease read the first draft of this book and gave me excellent comments on it. Phet Pease read the final draft and provided editorial comments that fine-tuned it. Gary's daughter, Tracy Holstad Conley used her talent and skill to create the cover for this book. Thank you all. This was truly a family project.

Acknowledgments

Dave and Jeff Pease were my technical team. Jeff formatted the final manuscript using software he developed. He enhanced photos, added captions and offered creative suggestions. Thank you for your many hours and your expertise Jeff. Dave was interested in this book from the beginning. He monitored my progress and created a proof copy of my first draft which made the project come alive. Dave took Jeff's final manuscript and prepared it for release to Amazon for distribution. Thank you for your encouragement and guidance Dave.

Carter Pease supported this project all the way. He listened to my frustrations as I tried to structure an outline into a readable story. He edited my drafts and provided insight into the character's dialog and the story as a whole. When I took a break from writing, he encouraged me to finish the project. He digitized and enhanced all of the photos. He also poured wine for our daily status update sessions which was essential! Thank you, Carter.

In writing this memoir, I referred to the following references. Most of these were written by family members. Thank you all!

- *A History of Rolla, North Dakota*, 1888-1988

- *A Jackson Tree*, William Jackson, 1955
- *An Olson Family Tree*, Ruth Olson, 1997
- *History of Rolette County North Dakota and Yarns of the Pioneers*, Laura Thompson Law, 1953
- *The Holstad Family History*, Don Limesand, 1992
- *Those Johnsons!* Jack and Penny Holstad, 2003

About the Author

Kathleen Holstad Pease retired from Qualcomm, Inc. as a Vice President of Engineering. She lives on an avocado/citrus acreage outside of San Diego with her husband Carter and their golden retriever Bailey. Their two sons and their families live in San Diego.

Kathleen enjoys creating art quilts, traveling, reading, writing, and spending time with friends and family. Some of her favorite moments are when the front door bursts open and her four grandsons run into the house with Bailey following close behind. For just a second, she can almost hear Grandpa Johnson shouting, "Don't let the kids bite the dog!"

Kathleen can be contacted at: kathy@kathypease.com

Made in the USA
Middletown, DE
16 May 2018

Pam Eddings

Thanks again for treating me & the girls to lunch when you were here. I just received my order of my new book today & I'm sending you a complimentary copy. Hope it will be a blessing to you. I will be taking my oldest son Russell & family to B.R. for Christmas. Will be first time all my siblings have been together for Christmas since 2001. Looking forward to it. Praying about attending BOTT this yr. Linda Rogers has invited me to stay w/ her. Will let you know. Love You,

Pam

It starts with a gift. It leads to transformed by Christ.

ANGEL TREE®
A Program of Prison Fellowship®

*For more information about Angel Tree,
visit us online at www.angeltree.org
or call us at 877-478-0100.*